1 PETER

J. Vernon McGee

THOMAS NELSON PUBLISHERS

Nashville

Published in Nashville, Tennessee, by Thomas Nelson, Inc., and distributed in Canada by Lawson Falle, Ltd., Cambridge, Ontario.

Quotations from *The Scofield Reference Bible*. Copyright 1909, 1917, renewed 1937, 1945 by Oxford University Press, Inc. Reprinted by permission.

Scripture quotations are from the KING JAMES VERSION of the Bible.

Library of Congress Cataloging-in-Publication Data

McGee, J. Vernon (John Vernon), 1904–1988
   [Thru the Bible with J. Vernon McGee]
   Thru the Bible commentary series / J. Vernon McGee.
     p.   cm.
   Reprint. Originally published: Thru the Bible with J. Vernon McGee. 1975.
   Includes bibliographical references.
   ISBN 0-8407-3307-0
   1. Bible—Commentaries. I. Title.
BS491.2.M37 1991
220.7'7—dc20   90–41340
                                           CIP

Printed in the United States of America
1 2 3 4 5 6 7 — 96 95 94 93 92 91

CONTENTS

1 PETER

PREFACE

The radio broadcasts of the Thru the Bible Radio five-year program were transcribed, edited, and published first in single-volume paperbacks to accommodate the radio audience.

There has been a minimal amount of further editing for this publication. Therefore, these messages are not the word-for-word recording of the taped messages which went out over the air. The changes were necessary to accommodate a reading audience rather than a listening audience.

These are popular messages, prepared originally for a radio audience. They should not be considered a commentary on the entire Bible in any sense of that term. These messages are devoid of any attempt to present a theological or technical commentary on the Bible. Behind these messages is a great deal of research and study in order to interpret the Bible from a popular rather than from a scholarly (and too-often boring) viewpoint.

We have definitely and deliberately attempted "to put the cookies on the bottom shelf so that the kiddies could get them."

The fact that these messages have been translated into many languages for radio broadcasting and have been received with enthusiasm reveals the need for a simple teaching of the whole Bible for the masses of the world.

I am indebted to many people and to many sources for bringing this volume into existence. I should express my especial thanks to my secretary, Gertrude Cutler, who supervised the editorial work; to Dr. Elliott R. Cole, my associate, who handled all the detailed work with the publishers; and finally, to my wife Ruth for tenaciously encouraging me from the beginning to put my notes and messages into printed form.

Solomon wrote, ". . . of making many books there is no end; and much study is a weariness of the flesh" (Eccl. 12:12). On a sea of books that flood the marketplace, we launch this series of THRU THE BIBLE with the hope that it might draw many to the one Book, *The Bible*.

J. VERNON MCGEE

1 PETER

The First Epistle of

PETER

INTRODUCTION

Simon Peter—"Peter, an apostle of Jesus Christ, to the strangers" (1 Pet.1:1).

Peter has been called the ignorant fisherman, but no man who had spent three years in the school of Jesus could be called ignorant. The Epistles of Peter confirm this. Peter deals with doctrine and handles weighty subjects. In the first few verses he deals with the great doctrines of election, foreknowledge, sanctification, obedience, the blood of Christ, the Trinity, the grace of God, salvation, revelation, glory, faith, and hope. My friend, you just couldn't have any more doctrine crowded into a few verses! The way in which he handles these great themes of the Bible reveals that he was by no means an ignorant fisherman.

A great change is seen in the life of Peter from these epistles. He had been impetuous, but now he is patient. He was bungling, fumbling, and stumbling when he first met Jesus. Our Lord told him in effect, "You are a pretty weak man now, but I am going to make you a Petros, a rock-man. And you will be built upon the foundation of Jesus Christ who is the Rock." Peter made it very clear that the Lord Jesus is the Rock on which the church is built. It is very interesting that although his name means "rock," he says that all believers are little rocks also: "Ye also, as lively stones, are built up a spiritual house" (1 Pet. 2:5). In other words, he is saying that every believer is a Peter. Simon Peter never takes an exalted position, as we shall see in his epistles. As he opens his epistle, he calls himself an apostle—he is just one of them. Although whenever the names of the apostles were enumerated, his was always first on the list, and although the Lord chose him to preach the first sermon on the Day of Pentecost, he did not feel that he was exalted above the others.

Peter wrote his epistles after Paul had written his epistles, somewhere between A.D. 64 and 67, after bloody Nero had come to the throne and persecution was already breaking out. According to tradition, Peter himself suffered martyrdom.

"The church that is at Babylon, elected together with you, saluteth you; and so doth Marcus my son" (1 Pet. 5:13). There are those who think that Babylon is used here in a symbolic manner or in a metaphorical sense and that Peter really meant Rome. However, there is no reason for him to use it in a metaphorical sense. Peter was an apostle who did not write in a symbolic manner such as we find used by John in the Book of Revelation. Peter writes very literally and practically. He gets down to where the rubber meets the road, right down on the asphalt of life. I believe that if he had meant Rome, he would have said Rome.

My own opinion is that Simon Peter never did go to Rome. I think he was in Asia Minor, the great heart of the Roman Empire, but he was not the apostle who opened up that territory. I think he followed Paul. Paul would not have gone to Rome if Peter had already been in Rome preaching the Gospel there, because Paul made it very clear that he went into places where the Gospel had not been preached before. Since Rome was on Paul's itinerary, it seems obvious that Paul, not Peter, founded the church at Rome.

Another very valid argument to indicate that Peter was in Babylon rather than Rome is based on the list of places which he addresses: "To the strangers scattered throughout Pontus, Galatia, Cappadocia, Asia, and Bithynia" (1 Pet. 1:1). All those places are in Asia Minor (the area which is called Turkey today). In listing them, he moves from east to west. This suggests that the writer was in the east at the time of writing. The natural and ordinary way to list geographical places is beginning from the point where you are. When I am in California and talk about going east, I would say that I am going through Arizona, Texas, and finally New York. It is normal to begin where I am and to name the places in sequence. Since Peter lists the places from east to west, it would seem logical that he was in literal Babylon.

After the Babylonian captivity, only a very small group of Jews returned to their land—actually there were fewer than sixty thousand. There was still a great colony of Jews in Babylon. Additional Jews had fled to Babylon when severe persecution began under Claudius in Rome. We know, for example, that Priscilla and Aquila fled to Corinth from Rome. Many others fled to Babylon. There was persecution both of Christians and of Jews. Since we know that the ministry of Peter was primarily to the Jews it seems most logical that he ministered to Jewish colonies in Asia Minor, and particularly in Babylon. Babylon was still a great city there on the Euphrates River, and many of the Jews had remained there after the end of the Captivity.

In spite of the fact that Papias mentions the death of Peter as occurring in Rome, there is no substantial historical basis for this supposition. I see no reason to discount the fact that Simon Peter was the apostle to those of the nation of Israel who were scattered abroad. I believe Peter went east while the apostle Paul went west.

The great theme of this epistle of Peter is Christian hope in the time of trial. Although Peter deals with great doctrines and handles weighty subjects, he doesn't write in a cold manner. Peter has been called the apostle of hope while Paul has been called the apostle of faith and John has been called the apostle of love. This epistle puts a great emphasis upon hope, but I believe that the word which conveys the theme of this epistle is *suffering*. Peter also emphasizes the grace of God, and some expositors feel it is his main emphasis. However, the word *suffering* or some cognate words that go with it occur in this epistle sixteen times. *Hope* is always tied with the suffering. Therefore, I think it is fair to say that the theme is the Christian hope in the time of trial.

Peter will have a great deal to say about the suffering of Christ. The suffering of Christ has been dealt with by the writer of the Hebrew epistle and by James in his epistle. Also the prophets certainly mentioned it. However, Peter will handle the subject a little differently.

Peter speaks out of a rich experience. Dr. Robert Leighton, in his book, *A Practical Commentary on First Peter*, makes a very timely comment that applies to Simon Peter. Let me share this with you because it is worth noting:

> . . . it is a cold and lifeless thing to speak of spiritual things on mere report; but when men can speak of them as their own—as having share and interest in them, and some experience of their sweetness—their discourse of them is enlivened with firm belief and ardent affection; they cannot mention them, but straight their hearts are taken with such gladness as they are forced to vent in praises.

For this reason, Simon Peter, while writing of suffering, emphasizes *joy!*

This leads me to say something very important regarding young preachers. In this day we have about us some very wonderful young expositors of the Word. I thank God for them. However, as I have listened to two or three of them, I feel very much as Dr. G. Campbell Morgan felt in his day. He and his wife went to hear a young preacher in whom they were particularly interested. He was eloquent, fine looking, and he delivered a great sermon. Afterward, on the way home, Mrs. Morgan was profuse in her praise and was surprised that Dr. Morgan made no response. Finally she asked, "Don't you think he is a great preacher?" He answered, "He will be after he suffers." Well, time went by, and this young man found out by experience what it cost to stand for Christ. He went through persecution; he experienced problems in his church; and one day he stood at an open grave as he buried one of his little children. Dr. Morgan and his wife went to hear him again because they loved this young man. After the service Mrs. Morgan asked, "Well, what do you think of him now?" Dr. Morgan answered, "He is a great preacher." You see, suffering had made the difference.

This has been my personal experience also. As a young preacher, I spoke a great deal about standing for the Lord and about suffering. I used to go to hospitals and pat people on the hand and pray with them. I would tell them that the Lord would be with them. At that time

I was a professional preacher, saying what I did not know to be true from my own experience, although I believed it. But the day came when I went into the hospital myself. Another preacher came in and prayed with me. When he started to go, I said to him, "I've done the same thing you have done. I've been here, and I have told people that God would be with them. Now you are going to walk out of here, but I am staying, and I will find out if it is a theory or if what I have been telling people is true." Friend, I found out it is true. Now it is no longer a mere theory. I know it by the fact that the Word of God says it and by the fact that I have experienced it. I don't argue with people about these things any more because there are certain things I know. I would never argue with you about whether honey is sweet or not. If you don't think it is sweet, that is your business. I had some this morning for breakfast, and I know it is sweet. That is the knowledge that comes from experience.

Simon Peter is not going to give us his theory of suffering. Simon Peter is going to speak to us out of his own tremendous experience, and it will become very wonderful to us as it becomes your experience and my experience.

OUTLINE

CHAPTER 1

THEME: Suffering and security produce joy; suffering and the Scriptures produce holiness

SUFFERING AND THE SECURITY OF BELIEVERS

A great many folk have never had the feeling of assurance in their salvation. The security of the believer is a doctrine which I believed, although it took me a long time to come to the place of assurance in my own salvation. And there are many folk who do not have the assurance of their salvation. Why? Because suffering and the security of the believer go together. And do you know what this produces? It produces *joy!* Can you imagine that?

Now this first verse is just loaded with meaning.

Peter, an apostle of Jesus Christ, to the strangers scattered throughout Pontus, Galatia, Cappadocia, Asia, and Bithynia [1 Pet. 1:1].

First of all, note his name: Peter, *Petros*, a stone. He is now the rockman. The Day of Pentecost is behind him, and he knows what it is to take a stand for Christ. He has been arrested and put in jail. He has been threatened, and he realizes that there is crucifixion on a cross ahead of him. Peter is a man who knows what he is talking about.

My friend, I must confess that I am not impressed by professors in theological seminaries, with little if any experience as pastors, who get up and spin off some little theory to prepare young men for the ministry. They don't really know the problems of a pastorate because they haven't had the experience. They don't know what it is really to suffer for Christ. After hearing them, I feel like turning back to Peter's first letter and reading it again, because I *believe* Peter—he knew what he was talking about. I'm sorry, but I don't trust these young professors. I want to hear from the man who has gone through the experiences.

"Peter, an apostle of Jesus Christ." Peter is an apostle of Jesus Christ—that is all he claimed to be. Although he always heads my list of apostles—I love him—he is not to be placed above the other apostles. When Paul went to Jerusalem to confer with the apostles, he talked with Peter, James, and John. He said that they seemed to be pillars of the church, but he did not learn the Gospel from them. Paul makes it very clear that he received the Gospel directly from Jesus Christ by revelation. Nowhere does Peter claim superiority. He was an apostle—that's all.

"To the strangers scattered throughout Pontus, Galatia, Cappadocia, Asia, and Bithynia." He is writing to the strangers, or aliens, who were scattered throughout the Roman Empire. They were Jews, called the *Diaspora* because they were no longer in the land of Palestine. Due to persecution and other reasons, they had settled throughout the empire. If you will check a map, you will find these places are all in Asia Minor, the area we know as Turkey today. You may recall that Paul on his second missionary journey tried to go into Bithynia, but the Spirit of God would not allow him to go there. It is my conviction that Simon Peter had already preached the Gospel there and that the Holy Spirit wanted Paul to go to people who had not heard the Gospel. Paul was the Apostle to the Gentiles, and Simon Peter was the apostle to Israelites who had turned to Christ.

Elect according to the foreknowledge of God the Father, through sanctification of the Spirit, unto obedience and sprinkling of the blood of Jesus Christ: Grace unto you, and peace, be multiplied [1 Pet. 1:2].

The apostle Peter immediately plunges us into deep doctrinal waters. For instance, he presents the doctrine of the Trinity: the foreknowledge of *God the Father*, sanctification of the *Spirit*, and sprinkling of the blood of *Jesus Christ*. My friend, don't let anyone tell you that the Bible does not teach the Trinity—the Bible is full of it! We certainly cannot consider Peter to be an ignorant fisherman, by the way, because he is talking about things that most of us do not know much about.

Theologians try to help us understand the tremendous doctrines of election and foreknowledge. For example, here is a statement from Lewis Sperry Chafer's *Systematic Theology:*

> Having recognized the sovereign right of God over His creation and having assigned to Him a rational purpose in all His plan, the truth contained in the doctrine of election follows in natural sequence as the necessary function of one who is divine (Vol. VII).

We must recognize that our God is a sovereign God and that this little universe is *His.* He created it. I don't know why He created it as He did, but since He is absolutely omniscient (knowing everything), and since He is omnipotent (having all power), and since He is sovereign, I conclude that He can do anything He wants to do that is consistent with His character.

He has a right to plan for the future. Apparently He did some planning. We call those plans the decrees that God had in His mind in the very beginning. That is to say, He had a plan that He was going to follow. He decreed to create the universe, and He did it. He never asked you or me about it. In fact, He has never asked me whether I wanted to be in existence. He could have left me out altogether. And He could have left you out, but He didn't! Thank God, He thought of you and me.

Also there was the decree to permit the fall of man. This, I think, took a great deal of planning on God's part, knowing that when He created the free moral agent called man, he would fall when given a free choice. Mankind chose to disobey God, but God had made arrangements for it. He had the decree to elect some to salvation, and He had the decree that He would send a Savior into the world. He certainly did that. He made a decree that He would save those who came to Him, the elect. You can call them anything you wish, but the people who turned to Christ for salvation are the elect. You may say, "Well, He didn't choose everybody." I don't find that in Scripture. The Lord Jesus said, "All that the Father giveth me shall come to me; and him that cometh to me I will in no wise cast out" (John 6:37). His invitation to "whosoever will" is, "Come unto me" (see Matt 11:28). It is a legitimate invitation to everyone, but there must be a response, and the response is your responsibility and my responsibility.

Peter really gets us into deep water when he says, "Elect according to the foreknowledge of God." You see, God is moving according to His plan. There must have been an infinite number of plans before Him, but He chose this one. Why? Because He knew it was the best possible plan, and little man is in no position to challenge His choice. He is the Creator, and we are only creatures. You and I didn't even determine the time we would be born, or the family into which we would come, or our height, or the color of our eyes, or our IQ. Whatever we are today is by the grace of God. He is the one who determined all of those things for us. They are all a part of His great plan.

I don't know why we find fault with God for having a plan. Perhaps some folk imagine that He is up to some dirty tricks—but He is not. Oh, my friend, God is good and gracious and long-suffering. He wants to save us, and He wants us to have happy lives. God is the one we can trust. How strange it is that some folk object to God's having a plan when they are perfectly happy to have men follow a plan.

For example, when my wife and I were to leave London, we boarded a plane that would bring us home to Los Angeles. When we were airborne, the captain talked to us on the intercom. I was happy to note that his voice sounded mature and that he spoke with assurance. I was sure he had flown that plane before. He outlined our flight plan, "We are going to fly over Scotland and over northern Ireland, and then we will cross the Atlantic. We will be going over Iceland, but we won't be able to see it because there are clouds over it. When we get to Greenland, I hope you will be able to see it. We may hit a little choppy weather there, but it's not bad. The cloud cover that is there now is breaking up. We will cross Hudson Bay and Labrador and will fly across those ice fields there. It looks like a very pleasant flight and a very smooth trip." You talk about foreknowledge and election! That whole trip was decided for us. And no one ran up to the cabin to protest, "You have no right to plan our trip!" We were delighted that he was following a plan.

My friend, I am sure glad that the God of this universe has a plan and that He knows what He is doing and where He is going and that He is doing the very best for us. I say hallelujah for election which is according to the foreknowledge of God. God is able to carry out His plan exactly because He knows everything. The pilot of the plane had gotten word about weather conditions, and his flight was plotted for him to follow—but it could have been upset. Not so with God's plan. Our God knows everything. He knows every condition; He knows everything that is foreseeable and unforeseeable. So you and I can trust Him implicitly. When Peter says, "Elect according to the foreknowledge of God," he is telling us what God the Father did.

Now he tells us about the work of the Holy Spirit: "through sanctification of the Spirit."

Let me remind you that when the word *sanctification* is identified with Christ, it means that *He* is our sanctification; we will never be any better, as far as our position is concerned, than we are at this moment because we are complete in Him, and we are accepted in the beloved. We cannot add to that; it is our position in Christ.

However, when the word *sanctification* is identified with the Holy Spirit, it means something else. When Peter says, "Through sanctification of the Spirit," he is talking about the ministry of the Holy Spirit in the world who not only converts us—is responsible for our New Birth—but He also begins to work in our lives to bring us up to the place of maturation where we become full, mature Christians. Unfortunately, there are many Christians who have been saved for fifty years or more and yet will be going into heaven as babes in Christ. They haven't matured at all. It will be embarrassing to go into the presence of God as still a burping baby! The work of the Holy Spirit is to sanctify us down here on this earth. How I wish there were more emphasis on that!

There are abroad in our land, at the time of this writing, at least twenty-five organizations or ministries which have become expert in telling you how to become an adequate Christian, a fulfilled Christian, and how you can be comfortable as a Christian. My friend, I hope you never get to the place where you do not feel your inadequacy and your dependence upon Jesus Christ as your Savior. I am tired of these "adequate" Christians. And some of them I meet convince me that I don't want to be "adequate," if that is adequateness! Now, please don't feel that I am being critical of one particular person or organization. I am simply insisting that the Word of God tells us that sanctification is by the Holy Spirit of God—not by some method of man's design.

Let me repeat that all of the Trinity is mentioned in this verse: "Elect according to the foreknowledge of God the Father"—He planned it; "through sanctification of the Spirit"—He protects us today; and it is through the "sprinkling of the blood of Jesus Christ"— personal application of the sacrifice of Christ on the cross, obedience.

Perhaps you are wondering how you can know if you are elect. Henry Ward Beecher divided folk into two categories: the "whosoever wills" and the "whosoever won'ts." You can know which one you are by making this simple test: Have you become obedient to Him? Is Christ really your Lord? If He is, you will love Him. The Lord Jesus said, "If you love me, keep my commandments." Do you do what you want to do and call that the will of God for your life? Or do you do what He wants you to do? If you are His, you will be obedient to Him.

"And sprinkling of the blood of Jesus Christ." There is often a silence about the blood of Christ, even in fundamental circles. As long as the blood of our Lord coursed through His veins, it had no saving value for us; but when that precious blood was shed, Christ Jesus gave His life. The life of the flesh is in the blood. He shed that blood that you and I might have life.

Remember that Peter is writing to Jews who had been brought up in Judaism. They were the *Diaspora*, believing Jews living in Asia Minor. They knew the Old Testament, and they understood that the high priest on the Day of Atonement took blood with him when he went into the Holy of Holies, and that he sprinkled the blood seven times on the mercy seat. Now the Lord Jesus Christ has taken His own blood to the throne of God (the throne at which we are judged as guilty sinners), and He sprinkled His blood there. He gave His life and paid the penalty for us. Now that throne of judgment is the throne of grace where you and I can come and receive salvation.

My friend, the Gospel has not been preached until the meaning of the blood of Christ has been explained. It may offend you aesthetically—the offense of the Cross is that He shed His blood. Of course it is not pretty, but your sin and my sin are not pretty either. Our ugly sin is what made it necessary for Christ to die for us.

This reminds me of a story about a terrible accident which occurred at a railroad crossing. Several people were killed when the train hit a car. There was a court trial, and the watchman who had been at the crossing at the time of the accident was questioned.

"Where were you at the time of the accident?"

"I was at the crossing."

"Did you have a lantern?."

"Yes."

"Did you wave that lantern to warn them of the danger?"

"I certainly did."

The court thought that was enough evidence. When the watchman walked out of the court he was heard to mumble to himself, "I'm sure glad they didn't ask me about the light in the lantern because the light had gone out."

My friend, there can be a lot of lanterns waved in the circles of fundamentalism and evangelicalism and conservatism. However, unless there is the message of the blood of Jesus Christ and the sprinkling of the blood which cleanses us from all sin, there is no light in the lantern. Now we come to one of the key words: "*Grace* unto you." Because of the work of the Trinity—God had you in mind, Christ died for you, and the *Holy Spirit* has come to indwell you to make you a better person—now God can save you by grace.

"Grace unto you and peace." Without the grace of God, you will never know the peace of God. I received a letter from a man in a cult which revealed that he didn't have peace. I can tell you right now that if you do not believe that Christ shed His blood for your sins, you will not have peace in your heart. You don't even need to tell me that you don't have peace. Peace and assurance and joy come when you know that your sins have been forgiven.

Simon Peter is not waving a lantern that has no light. He is not talking about something that is purely theoretical. This rugged fisherman knows grace and peace through the blood of Christ because Jesus Himself told him about it. He knows it because he had seen Jesus die;

he saw where He had been buried, and he saw the resurrected Christ. The old wishy-washy, mollycoddling, shilly-shally man has now become a rock-man. He could stand at the Day of Pentecost and preach about Christ's death and resurrection. He could go to jail, be persecuted, write an epistle like this, and finally be crucified for the Gospel.

Now, after spending some time considering the second verse of Peter's epistle, I am sure you will agree with me that Peter was not an ignorant fisherman, by any means. He has been dealing with the tremendous doctrines of election, foreknowledge, foreordination, and predestination. All of these great concepts are on God's side of the fence, and none of us can come up with a final explanation. We are dealing with an infinite God who knows everything. His foreknowledge means that He knows every plan that is imaginable, and He knows exactly what He is going to do. We call that foreordination. At this point, let me give you another statement, which is a good one, from Dr. Lewis Sperry Chafer's Systematic Theology:

> . . . foreknowledge in God is that which He Himself purposes to bring to pass. In this way, then, the whole order of events from the least detail unto the greatest operates under the determining decree of God so as to take place according to His sovereign purpose. By so much, divine foreknowledge is closely related to foreordination. Likewise, foreknowledge in God should be distinguished from omniscience in that the latter is extended sufficiently to embrace all things past, present, and future, while foreknowledge anticipates only the future events (Vol. VI).

My friend, let me repeat that we are dealing with an infinite God. You and I have a little, finite mind. I am told that if a brain weighs eight ounces, it is pretty heavy. But I don't believe that an eight-ounce brain can comprehend the infinite God of the universe. Since He is omniscient, knowing everything that is possible to know—everything that is happening and everything that could happen—I am trusting Him and I intend to continue in that direction.

Now in the next verse Peter looks back to the past.

Blessed be the God and Father of our Lord Jesus Christ, which according to his abundant mercy hath begotten us again unto a lively hope by the resurrection of Jesus Christ from the dead [1 Pet. 1:3].

The word blessed, which is used here, is a different word from the blessed that is used in the Sermon on the Mount. The word used here is the Greek word from which we derive our word eulogy. It means "to praise." In the New Testament this word is never used in reference to man. God does not praise man, but man is to praise God, and He is the Father.

In our culture today we hear the fathers praising their sons. It isn't very often that we find a son praising his father. But we are to praise God the Father.

"The God and Father of our Lord Jesus Christ." He is the Father of our Lord Jesus Christ in a unique way. Remember that the Lord Jesus made this distinction when He spoke to Mary Magdalene on the morning of His resurrection: ". . . I ascend unto my Father, and your Father; and to my God, and your God" (John 20:17). He is the Father of the Lord Jesus Christ because of His position in the Trinity. They are equal. But you and I do not call Him Father, except on the basis that Peter mentions here: He has begotten us. The word begotten has to do with the regenerating work of the Holy Spirit.

"Hath begotten us again unto a living hope." (I have substituted the word living for the Old English word lively.) You and I have a living hope, a hope that rests upon the fact of the resurrection of Jesus Christ from the dead. And since Christ was raised from the dead by the Spirit of God, this is a further reference to the Holy Spirit.

This is a paean of praise to the Trinity. This is our song because we have been begotten, born again, as we shall see in verse 23, "not of corruptible seed, but of incorruptible, by the word of God, which liveth and abideth for ever."

Notice that the living hope we have rests upon the blood of Christ. A body without blood is a dead body—it has to be. If it is a living body, it will have blood coursing through it. You and I today have a living hope because of the blood of Christ shed for us. He died that you and I might live—because He paid our penalty. It is "a living hope by the resurrection of Jesus Christ from the dead."

Peter emphasizes the resurrection of Christ. The Resurrection was his great theme on the Day of Pentecost and in all of his messages. He said in effect, "All that you have seen here today is because Jesus whom you crucified has come back from the dead." And when he writes his epistles, he anchors them in the resurrection of Christ.

Paul does the same thing. He tells us that Jesus Christ was delivered for our offenses; He died for our sins. But He was raised for our justification, that we might be in Christ, accepted in the beloved, able to stand before God. He doesn't simply subtract sin from us; He makes over to us His righteousness. We stand before God in the righteousness of Jesus Christ.

Peter has described to us what God has done for us in the past. Now he moves into the future.

To an inheritance incorruptible, and undefiled, and that fadeth not away, reserved in heaven for you [1 Pet. 1:4].

"An inheritance incorruptible," meaning that it is nondestructible. It cannot be damaged in any way—no rust, no moth, no germ, no fire can touch it.

"Undefiled" indicates that it is not stained or defiled by anything. We will not get this inheritance illegally.

"That fadeth not away." We won't inherit it and then find it to be worthless, like some stock that once had value and then became completely valueless.

"Reserved in heaven for you." The word *reserved* means it is guarded. God the Father, God the Son, and God the Holy Spirit are taking care of it for us. We couldn't have it in a better safety deposit box than that!

I heard of a man who was willed a beautiful Southern home in Louisiana, but the very night the original owner died, the house caught on fire and burned down—and there was no insurance. The wonderful home that he was to inherit went up in smoke.

My friend, as believers, we have an inheritance that is incorruptible. This is a wonderful thing to look forward to!

It will help us to appreciate this verse if we remember that Peter had in mind Jewish Christians who were suffering trial and persecution for their faith. They had been forced to leave their homelands and whatever inheritance would have been theirs. Their ancestors had been delivered out of Egypt, and all through the wilderness wanderings they had the hope of the Promised Land before them. They praised God as the Creator of the world and as their Redeemer from Egypt. However, the believers to whom Peter was writing (and you and I as well) praise God as the Father of the incarnate Son, the Lord Jesus, the Author of the new creation and of a spiritual redemption. Also, He gives a living hope, a hope that will never die. He has begotten us and made us His sons through the regenerating work of the Holy Spirit. And in addition He has reserved for us an inheritance—not on earth but an inheritance in heaven. That inheritance is imperishable, indestructible, and no enemy can take it away from us. Someone has expressed it poetically:

It will always be new; it will never decay.
No night ever comes; it will always be day.

How it gladdens my heart with joy that's untold
To think of that land where nothing grows old.

Unfortunately, in our day our attention has been taken away from that which is future because so much emphasis is placed on the present.

Who are kept by the power of God through faith unto salvation ready to be revealed in the last time [1 Pet. 1:5].

"Kept by the power of God" emphasizes the keeping power of God. Kept is probably one of the most wonderful words we have here—"kept by the power of God through faith."

The story is told of a Scotsman, who was typically economical, leaving instructions that only one word should be engraved upon his tombstone. But that one word, taken from this verse, is one of the greatest I know. It was the single word *KEPT*. He was "kept by the power of God through faith unto salvation ready to be revealed in the last time."

The apostle Paul said the same thing: "Being confident of this very thing that he which hath begun a good work in you will perform it until the day of Jesus Christ" (Phil. 1:6). My friend, do you think He can keep you? Oh, I am weary of the emphasis being put on the work of the flesh. We are being told that if we follow some little set of rules, we can become "adequate Christians." I wonder if the fellows who are giving all these messages have reached some celestial level which the rest of us have not been able to attain. They ask, "Are you sufficient, are you satisfied?" My answer is, "No—I am pressing on the upward way, I am pressing toward the mark for the prize of the high calling of God in Christ Jesus. I am not satisfied. I have not found life sufficient." My friend, let me add a strong statement that may startle you: *You cannot live the Christian life!* Perhaps you are asking, "Do you really mean that?" Yes, I do. I would challenge you to show me a verse or any Scripture where God has asked you to live the Christian life. He has never done that. I have an old nature, and that old nature will be with me as long as I am on this earth. Sometimes that old nature really shows. I have a bad temper that flares at times. I say things even to my wonderful wife so that I must go later and make up with her. I take her in my arms and tell her I'm sorry for what I said. She forgives me, and it is always wonderful to make up, you know. However I still have an old nature—and you do too. And neither of us can change our old natures by trying to follow a little set of rules. We can no more change that old nature than we can take a gallon of perfume out to the barnyard, pour it on a pile of manure, and make it as fragrant as a bed of roses. My friend, you have that old nature, and you cannot change it.

The only way in the world that you can live the Christian life is by the power of the Holy Spirit and by the fact that you are kept by the power of God—right on through until the day when you will be delivered to Him in heaven. As we are going to see, it all has to do with a personal relationship with Jesus Christ.

We come now to the key verse of this epistle—

Wherein ye greatly rejoice, though now for a season, if need be, ye are in heaviness through manifold temptations [1 Pet. 1:6].

The suffering and the security of the believer produce—of all things—joy! They can do that because of the work of the Triune God. God our Father, according to His mercy—oh, He has been so merciful!—has begotten us, given us a new nature and a living hope by the resurrection of Jesus Christ from the dead. And out yonder in the future He has a marvelous inheritance waiting for us.

"Wherein ye greatly rejoice." Rejoice in what? In something good? No, "in heaviness through manifold trials." This places in contrast two words that are worlds apart: rejoice and trials.

Peter gives us reasons for enduring trials down here in this life. "Now for a season"—the trials will not be long, compared to eternity. In our day there is too much emphasis on the present life. Psychology and materialism have slipped into the church. We are told that we must develop ourselves into a full-orbed individual. If we are having trouble, something is wrong with our Christianity. Oh, my friend, it doesn't mean that at all!

Instead of so much introspection, we ought to be looking outward to the great God we have and to the marvelous inheritance which He has ready for us to receive some day. We should stop this attempt to improve our old nature through the power of the flesh. God is the one who is in the business of improving us. He is the one who is trying to bring us to a maturity in our Christian life. God's way of improving us is through manifold trials.

We have been told this in previous books—in fact, it is almost like a stuck recording. Jesus told us not to be dismayed. He said that in the world we would have troubles. In the Epistle to the Hebrews we learned that God tests us by trials and troubles. James wrote about the testings that come from God. And Paul had a great deal to say about suffering. Now Peter comes along and says the same thing.

I know it is not at all popular to teach that God will prove us and lead us on to maturity through suffering. People would rather be encouraged to think that they are somebody important and that they can do great things on their own. My friend, we are nothing until the Spirit of God begins to move in our hearts and lives. We have nothing to offer to God. He has everything to offer to us.

We need always to remember that our trials are only temporary. Paul says the same thing: "For our light affliction, which is but for a moment, worketh for us a far more exceeding and eternal weight of glory; while we look not at the things which are seen, but at the things which are not seen: for the things which are seen are temporal; but the things which are not seen are eternal" (2 Cor. 4:17–18).

The things at our fingertips which we consider so valuable are not really of value. They are simply passing things when measured in the perspective of eternity. All these things are destructible. They are corruptible, and they can be defiled. The things of this world do fade away. The things we cannot see are the eternal things. They are of real value.

> **That the trial of your faith, being much more precious than of gold that perisheth, though it be tried with fire, might be found unto praise and honour and glory at the appearing of Jesus Christ [1 Pet. 1:7].**

Peter uses here a very apt illustration, and he uses a wonderful word: precious. A dear lady of my acquaintance, a real saint of God up in her seventies, really overworks this word precious. Everything is precious to her. She has told me that I am precious and my radio program is precious. She told me that something I had said was precious. People had given her a gift and that was precious, and she says she had a precious time visiting with her friends, and they had a precious meal together. Well, precious is a woman's word, but notice who uses it here—Simon Peter, that great, big, rugged fisherman. He speaks of the trial of our faith being precious. And he uses the word precious seven times, as we shall see.

"The trial of your faith, being much more precious than of gold."

After gold is mined, it is put into a smelter, a red-hot furnace. The purpose is not to destroy the gold; it is to purify the gold. When the gold is melted, the dross is drawn off to get the pure gold. Later on, Peter will also make an application of this regarding the suffering of our Lord. He says that we have been redeemed, not with gold or silver, but with something infinitely more precious than that—the blood of Christ.

When God tests us today, He puts us into the furnace. He doesn't do that to destroy us or to hurt or harm us. But He wants pure gold, and that is the way He will get it. Friend, that is what develops Christian character. At the time of testing, the dross is drawn off and the precious gold appears. That is God's method. That is God's school.

We don't hear that teaching very much in our day. Rather, we are being taught to become sufficient within ourselves. Oh, my friend, you and I are not adequate; we are not sufficient, and we never will be. We simply come to God as sinners, and He saves us by His grace through the blood of Christ. Then He wants to live His life through us. He tries to teach us this through our trials. He is drawing us closer to Him.

There are no shortcuts to maturity. All the gimmicks and new methods will lead to a dead-end street. The only thing that will bring us into a true maturation is the trial of our faith which God sends to us.

"At the appearing of Jesus Christ." I believe that at the appearing of Jesus Christ, we will thank God for our trials—in fact, we may wish we had experienced more of them because, when we are in His presence, we will see the value of them. Just think of the trials the apostles went through! Simon Peter, when he wrote this epistle, knew that crucifixion was ahead of him. He says that the trials are going to bring out the gold when we appear in Christ's presence. That's the thing toward which we are to look forward.

Now Simon Peter will say something very precious—

Whom having not seen, ye love; in whom, though now ye see him not, yet believing, ye rejoice with joy unspeakable and full of glory [1 Pet. 1:8].

This verse ought to mean a great deal to us. Remember that Peter had seen the Lord Jesus personally and had traveled with Him for three years. He had failed miserably during that period. Then one morning on the shore of the Sea of Galilee, the Lord prepared breakfast for the men who had been fishing all night, and I guess He was waiting for Peter. I would have expected Him to say, "Peter, I can't trust you. Why did you deny Me? I'm going to have to put you on the sidelines. I cannot use you." But no, He didn't say that. Rather, He said, "Simon, son of Jonas, lovest thou me?" (see John 21:17). That was His question: Do you love Me? The man who had been a braggadocio before was no longer bragging. He finally just cried out, "Lord, You know all things; You know that I love You." And the Lord Jesus said, "I'm going to let you feed My sheep" (see John 21:16–17). And it was Peter who preached the first sermon on the Day of Pentecost. Now Peter says to you and me, "Whom having not seen, ye love." The Holy Spirit is the one who can make Him real to you and me. My friend, this is the secret of the Christian life. When we *love* Him, everything else falls into place. If you do not love Him, no course in the world is going to help you. And neither will He commission you to feed His sheep.

"Though now ye see him not yet believing, ye rejoice with joy unspeakable and full of glory." Does this set your heart to beating faster? Are you really in love with Him, or do you have a dead religion that is quite meaningless? Oh, my friend, Christ is so wonderful! Simon Peter loved Him. Paul loved Him, and all of those who have genuinely served Him have loved Him. I hope you love Him today. If you do, it will solve a lot of your problems. It will help the husband-wife relationship. It is wonderful how the love of Christ draws our hearts together. Not only will it help you in your home, it will help you in your church. Loving Christ draws believers together. It will help you in all your relationships if you love Him.

"Ye rejoice with joy unspeakable and full of glory." Loving Christ brings rejoicing to your heart. Are you a rejoicing Christian, my friend? You should be. You are a child of the King, and you have an inheritance coming to you some day. How wonderful it is to be His child!

Receiving the end of your faith, even the salvation of your souls [1 Pet. 1:9].

Salvation was a subject of prophecy in the Old Testament. Both the prophets and apostles bore witness to the truth of it. What an encouragement that was to the *Diaspora*, those who were suffering for their faith.

SUFFERING AND THE SCRIPTURES

Of which salvation the prophets have inquired and searched diligently, who prophesied of the grace that should come unto you [1 Pet. 1:10].

All the prophets prophesied diligently concerning it.

Searching what, or what manner of time the Spirit of Christ which was in them did signify, when it testified beforehand the sufferings of Christ, and the glory that should follow [1 Pet. 1:11].

The prophets spoke of "the sufferings of Christ" and the grace of God. We find this in Isaiah 53 and in Psalm 22 as well as in many other Scriptures.

"And the glory that should follow" is found, for example, in Isaiah 11 and Psalm 45. The prophets all spoke of Christ's suffering and of the sovereignty and of the glory that is to come when Christ comes as King to the earth to establish His kingdom.

"The Spirit of Christ which was in them did signify." This tells us specifically that the prophets of the Old Testament wrote by the Spirit of Christ. This is one of the many statements contained in the Word of God declaring that the Old Testament was inspired of God. These men wrote by the "Spirit of Christ."

The prophets wrote some things which they themselves did not grasp. They searched for the meaning diligently, "searching what, or what manner of time the Spirit of Christ which was in them did signify, when it testified beforehand the sufferings of Christ, and the glory that should follow." There are many places in the Old Testament that speak of the suffering of Christ, and there are many other places that speak of the sovereignty of Christ, of the kingdom age. Grace and glory are combined, and it was difficult for them to understand this. For example, Isaiah wrote in the fifty-third chapter of the sufferings of Christ; then in the eleventh chapter he wrote of the Messiah coming in power and glory to the earth to establish His kingdom. This seeming contradiction was very puzzling to the prophets, and they tried to find out how both could be true. As the prophets looked down the corridors of time they saw these two events as two great mountain peaks, but they could not see the valley of time between them.

You and I are in the unique position of living in that interval of time between the suffering of Christ, which is in the past, and the glory of Christ, which is yet in the future.

It will help you to understand the prophecies of the suffering and sovereignty of Christ if you picture the two events as two great mountain peaks. Here in Pasadena we have a backdrop of the Sierra Madre mountains. As the crow flies, they are about five miles away, but driving the winding road to get there makes them about twenty-five miles away. Mount Wilson is in the foreground and is approximately six thousand feet high. Behind that peak we can see another peak, Mount Waterman, which looks as if it is the same height as Mount Wilson. Actually, Mount Waterman is over eight thousand feet high. However, it looks as if they are the same height and that they are right together. In actual fact, they are not together at all. A tremendous valley separates them—between twenty-five and thirty-five miles across—and I estimate that it is probably fifty miles from one mountain peak to the other. Yet, seeing them from a distance, you would think they were right together.

In just such a way, the prophets looking into the future saw the suffering of Christ and the glory of Christ as two mountain peaks, which appeared to be right together. I am of the opinion that there were sceptics and higher critics in those days who argued, "This is a conflict; the Scriptures are in contradiction. You cannot have it both ways.

Either He comes in suffering or He comes to reign." Of course we know now that both are true. And the valley between is the church age, which already is approaching two thousand years in length.

Unto whom it was revealed, that not unto themselves, but unto us they did minister the things, which are now reported unto you by them that have preached the gospel unto you with the Holy Ghost sent down from heaven; which things the angels desire to look into [1 Pet. 1:12].

Now the apostles are saying, "We are preaching the same thing that the prophets did." The only difference was that the prophets could not make the distinction between Christ's suffering and glory while the apostles were in the position of being able to understand the distinction.

"Which things the angels desire to look into." It is my opinion that the angels, God's created intelligences, are standing up yonder looking at you and me wondering why we don't get busy and give out this tremendous message today. They desire to do it themselves. They would love to come and proclaim it to the world. You recall that the angel Gabriel came and made the announcement to Mary and later to Joseph that Jesus was to be born. Also, he came to tell Zacharias that he was going to have a son, named John, who would be the forerunner of the Messiah. I am sure that Gabriel would love to come down again and say to me as I make my radio broadcast, "Move over, McGee, you are not putting enough into it. This thing is lots more wonderful than you are making it!" Although he would like to come down, God won't let him. He says to Gabriel, "No, I've got to use that poor instrument,

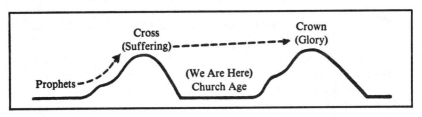

McGee." Today he is using *human* instruments to get out His Word, because we are not living in the day of the ministry of angels. We are living in the day of the ministry of the Holy Spirit. As children of God we are indwelt by the Holy Spirit—". . . if any man have not the Spirit of Christ, he is none of his" (Rom. 8:9). If you are Christ's, you are indwelt by the Spirit of God.

Now, do you think that an angel could do something for you that the Spirit of God could not do? No. We are living in the day of the ministry of the Holy Spirit, the day of grace, when the Spirit of God takes the things of Christ and reveals them unto us. What are we to do in light of this?

> **Wherefore gird up the loins of your mind, be sober, and hope to the end for the grace that is to be brought unto you at the revelation of Jesus Christ [1 Pet. 1:13].**

"Gird up the loins of your mind." This is a figure of speech based on the gathering and fastening up of the long Eastern garments so that they would not interfere with the wearer's vigorous movements. It was an expression that was understood in Peter's day, but I would like to bring it down to good old Americana. I think we would say, "Get with it!" Or maybe we would say, "Get turned on!"

"Be sober." You won't need drugs; you won't need alcohol. Let the Word of God turn you on. However, "be sober" means more than this. It means to be sober minded, to adopt a serious attitude in the study of the Word of God.

"And hope to the end." This is the great epistle of hope. Why (as we have already seen) should the child of God be willing to endure trials? Because we have a hope, and that hope rests upon the resurrection of Jesus Christ.

"The grace that is to be brought unto you at the revelation of Jesus Christ." At the time when the Lord Jesus comes to take the church out of the world, He will bring plenty of grace with Him. By His grace, He will take out *every* believer. And each believer's works are to be judged at Christ's judgment seat (*Bēma Seat*). At that time we will either suffer loss or receive a reward—and that certainly will be by His grace!

The fact that we will be judged someday is another incentive to endure the trials of this world. How we live down here upon this earth is very important. Today believers are confronted with the demand to lead transformed lives which only the Word of God can produce in us. One of the reasons God lets us go through trials and troubles is because He wants to fashion us according to His plan. We are to yield to Him in all our tribulations.

As obedient children, not fashioning yourselves according to the former lusts in your ignorance [1 Pet. 1:14].

"As obedient children." The Scriptures will lead us to obedience. You may recall that James said, "Be ye doers of the word, and not hearers only . . ." (James 1:22). The Word of God not only brings us hope, but it also leads to our obedience. The Word of God is to be obeyed; we are to yield to its instruction.

While I was ill, several folk sent copies of this poem by Alice Hansche Mortenson, which was a great comfort to me:

I NEEDED THE QUIET

I needed the quiet so He drew me aside,
Into the shadows where we could confide.

Away from the bustle where all the day long
I hurried and worried when active and strong.

I needed the quiet though at first I rebelled
But gently, so gently, my cross He upheld,

And whispered so sweetly of spiritual things
Though weakened in body, my spirit took wings

To heights never dreamed of when active and gay.
He loved me so greatly He drew me away.

I needed the quiet. No prison my bed,
But a beautiful valley of blessings instead—

A place to grow richer in Jesus to hide.
I needed the quiet so He drew me aside.

Why did He draw me aside? So that I might spend time in the Word of God. Oh, how important it is in the lives of believers!

"Not fashioning yourselves according to the former lusts in your ignorance"—that is, not conforming your behavior to what it used to be before you knew better. We are to live lives which reveal that we have been transformed from the inside. We are not to walk around with an artificial smile on our face like a floorwalker at Macy's who acts as if he is delighted to serve you when in reality his corns are killing him and he wishes you would go home and stay home. We are not to be artificial. We are to so yield to God that we will be genuinely transformed.

But as he which hath called you is holy, so be ye holy in all manner of conversation [1 Pet. 1:15].

Holiness is something that is really misunderstood. To the average person, holiness means to assume a very pious attitude, to become almost abnormal in everyday life. It is thought to be a superficial thing.

My friend, the Lord wants you to be a fully integrated personality. He wants you to enjoy life and have fun—I don't mean the sinful kind of fun, but real delight and enjoyment in the life He has given to you. Holiness is to the spiritual life what health is to the physical life. You like to see a person who is physically fine, robust, and healthy. Well, holiness is to be healthy and robust spiritually. Oh, how we need folk like this today!

Because it is written, Be ye holy; for I am holy [1 Pet. 1:16].

Is our holiness to be an attribute like God's holiness? No. Our God is absolutely perfect, and we will never, while we are in this life, reach that state. Oh, I have met several folk who thought they had reached that state, but I could not find anyone who would agree with them that they had reached that exalted level. Then what does it mean to be holy as God is holy?

Our God is a complete, wonderful personality. Although you and I are mere human beings, we can be full grown; we can reach maturation. A beautiful little baby in a crib may win a blue ribbon, but if he is still a little baby in a crib seventeen years later, something is wrong. He should be a healthy young fellow turning out for football practice. As Christians, we should be growing spiritually like that. What can produce this kind of growth? The Word of God.

And if ye call on the Father, who without respect of persons judgeth according to every man's work, pass the time of your sojourning here in fear [1 Pet. 1:17].

"Without respect of persons" means without partiality. God judges every man's work impartially. God doesn't have little pets. God is going to judge the work of every Christian fairly. This has nothing to do with your salvation; it has everything to do with the kind of life you are living down here on this earth. The fact that God is going to judge us ought to cause us to become very sober minded and to give a little more attention to the life that we are living. My friend, let's make sure that we are not superficial. Are you trying to keep a smile on your face and radiate happiness and sunshine everywhere you go? The Gospel does not sprinkle rosewater on a bunch of dead weeds. The Gospel *transforms* lives and brings with it a living hope which rests upon the resurrection of Christ. Believers have *life* from the living Savior who is up yonder at God's right hand.

Forasmuch as ye know that ye were not redeemed with corruptible things, as silver and gold, from your vain conversation received by tradition from your fathers;

But with the precious blood of Christ, as of a lamb without blemish and without spot [1 Pet. 1:18–19].

"Forasmuch as ye know"—and I hope you know that you have been redeemed.

In these verses Peter is speaking of the objective work of God for your salvation, which is redemption. My friend, He had to pay a price for you. You and I stood under the judgment of God, for the Scripture says ". . . the soul that sinneth, it shall die" (Ezek. 18:4). God has never revoked that decree. God never changes. He is the same yesterday, today, and forever. The immutability of God is the terror of the wicked—if they give any thought to it at all. We hear it said that we are living in a new age with new thoughts and new values, but God has not changed. There would be no reason for Him to change because He knew the end from the beginning. Neither did He learn anything when He looked at the morning newspaper or heard the television newscaster this morning. It didn't give Him any information because He knows all things—past, present, and future. And God has not changed His decree that "the soul that sinneth, it shall die."

"Ye were not redeemed with corruptible things, as silver and gold." Although silver and gold can be purified by being put into a crucible—heated red-hot so the dross can be drawn off—even they will corrupt in time. If you have table service of silver which you use only for guests, you know that whenever you bring it out, it is tarnished and looks like pewter. It is corrupting. Silver and gold are perishable. We are not redeemed with corruptible things.

"From your vain conversation received by tradition from your fathers." Life is vain; that is, it is empty without the redemption of Christ. There is nothing quite so meaningless as human life apart from the redemption of Christ. Everything else in this world serves a purpose. Every animal and every plant on this earth serves a purpose. The sun, the moon, and every star in the sky serves a purpose. But man without God is meaningless. Someone has said that mankind is just a rash on the epidermis of a minor planet! Well, that's about all man is apart from God. We have not been redeemed by corruptible things—not anything from this empty life. Man has nothing to offer to God for his own redemption. My friend, what do you have that God needs?

God taught me how unimportant I was one summer when He put me flat on my back. I was scheduled to conduct Bible conferences in the Northwest, and I thought they were important. God said to me something like this, "Listen, I got along without you before you got here, and I'm going to get along without you after you leave. You think that speaking at those conferences is important, but I want you to learn what is important. I want you to lie here flat on your back and look up to Me to find out that your relationship with Me is the most important thing there is. I have some things to teach you. Sometimes when you teach My Word, you teach way out ahead of where you are living. I want you to find out that what I say in My Word is true, and a little suffering isn't going to hurt you at all. It is going to mold you and shape you the way I want you to be." My friend, I learned that I have nothing that God needs.

What can you or I do today to redeem ourselves? *Nothing!* Then how can we be redeemed?

"With the precious blood of Christ." Here again Simon Peter, that rugged fisherman, says that the blood of Christ is precious. As I have said before the blood of Christ is not mentioned in some religious circles. The words are omitted from the hymnals of many liberal churches. Their reasoning is that the blood is crude. Well, I don't think it is crude, and certainly Simon Peter didn't think it was crude. He said it was precious.

"With the precious blood of Christ, as of a lamb without blemish and without spot." Simon Peter, who lived with Jesus Christ for three years, said that He was without blemish and without spot. He was absolutely sinless. I will take Peter's word for it—certainly he is in a better position to judge than modern authors who depict Jesus as just another sinful man. The modern authors write for money, but Simon Peter wasn't in the moneymaking business. All he got for his witness of Christ was suffering and finally crucifixion. He said that we were not redeemed with corruptible things, as silver and gold, "but with the precious blood of Christ, as of a lamb without blemish and without spot." This is an objective statement of our redemption. This is what God did for you and me.

Who verily was foreordained before the foundation of the world, but was manifest in these last times for you [1 Pet. 1:20].

"Who verily was foreordained"—a better word is *foreknown*. Christ was foreknown before the foundation of the world.

Now let me give you a tremendous statement from *The Scofield Reference Bible* (p. 1333):

> The sovereign choice of God in foreordination, election, and predestination logically originated in the divine decision based on His eternal omniscience of all possible plans of action. The order logically, not chronologically, is omniscience, divine decision (foreordination, election, predestination), and foreknowledge. As God's decision is eternal, however, so also His foreknowledge is eternal. As foreknowledge extends to all events, it includes all that is embraced in election, foreordination, and predestination. Election is, therefore, according to foreknowledge, and foreknowledge is according to election, meaning that both are in perfect agreement.

When we begin to deal with words like *foreordination, election, predestination, foreknowledge,* etc., I feel that we, with our finite minds, treat God as if He were a great big computer. He isn't that at all. He has a heart bigger than the whole universe. When I was in seminary studying theology, it seemed pretty important to know whether or not foreknowledge comes before foreordination; but, frankly, since that time I have not been concerned with which comes first. I realize now that the important thing is that Christ was "foreknown before the foundation of the world, but was manifest in these last times for you." To put it very simply, the Cross of Christ was not an ambulance sent to a wreck. Christ was the Lamb who was slain before the foundation of the world because God knew all the time that Vernon McGee would need a Savior, and He loved him enough to provide that Savior. I don't need a computer to go over this. I only need a God with a great big heart of love who provided redemption by His grace.

Who by him do believe in God, that raised him up from the dead, and gave him glory; that your faith and hope might be in God [1 Pet. 1:21].

"That raised him up from the dead"—Simon Peter keeps reminding us of the resurrection of Christ.

"That your faith and hope might be in God." Previously he put together the words *grace* and *hope;* now it is faith and hope. Peter is the great apostle of hope, and hope rests upon the resurrection of Christ and upon the fact that we have a living Savior who will be returning some day.

> **Seeing ye have purified your souls in obeying the truth through the Spirit unto unfeigned love of the brethren, see that ye love one another with a pure heart fervently [1 Pet. 1:22].**

"Seeing ye have purified your souls in obeying the truth through the Spirit." The Word of God is a miracle cleansing agent. On television today advertisers make great claims for their soaps and other cleansing agents. They tell us how superior their product is over the products of their competitors. All of them are trying to sell a "miracle" product. My friend, the only true miracle cleanser in this world is the Word of God. It is the best bar of soap that you can get. The Word of God will really take spots out, and many of us need to get closer to it.

"Unto unfeigned love of the brethren see that ye love one another with a pure heart fervently." Your relationship to the Word of God will lead you to a right relationship with other believers.

> **Being born again, not of corruptible seed, but of incorruptible, by the word of God, which liveth and abideth for ever [1 Pet. 1:23].**

Peter brings us back to the Word of God again. He is talking now about the subjective work of God in salvation. We have seen that the objective work of God was that Christ died—that's our redemption. It happened over nineteen hundred years ago, and we can't add anything to it. However, if you are to become a child of God, you must be born again, born from above. This, you recall, is what the Lord Jesus said to Nicodemus, as recorded in John 3:3. Nicodemus was a man who was religious to his fingertips, yet the Lord Jesus told him that he must be born *anothen*, meaning "from above," by the Spirit of God.

"Not of corruptible seed but of incorruptible, by the word of God, which liveth and abideth for ever." You cannot be saved, you cannot be born again apart from the Word of God. This Book is the miracle that is in the world today. Although I believe this, I never cease to marvel at the letters I receive from folk who tell me that they have been born again and their lives have been transformed from listening to my Bible-teaching radio broadcast. It is wonderful, but I don't understand how it happens; I only know that it is the result of the Word of God which liveth and abideth for ever.

We are living in a day when a great deal is said about virility. Men want to be vigorous and virile; women want to be sexy. Much emphasis is put upon that today. I hope you won't misunderstand when I say to you that if you want something that is virile and vigorous and sexy in a proper sense, turn to the Word of God. It is full of life, and it is life-giving. Put your arms around the Savior by putting your trust in Him, and a new birth will take place. There will be a miraculous birth because the Word of God is virile and vigorous, and it can penetrate your heart and make you a child of God. Oh, my friend, how important this is! Yet people are so preoccupied with sex and virility that they miss it. They are running around after emptiness. Sometimes I think that the whole human race is becoming obsessed with it. You would think that this generation had discovered sex! If they would only realize that the thing that really brings a birth within us is the Word of God as it reveals Christ to us. Then something tremendous takes place within us, and we are *born again!*

> **For all flesh is as grass, and all the glory of man as the flower of grass. The grass withereth, and the flower thereof falleth away [1 Pet. 1:24].**

Don't ever think that there is something of value in us that we can offer to God. All the glory of mankind is like the fragile flower of grass. In other words, mankind is like the grass which I can see from my window. It is nice and green in the summertime, but it is brown and dead in the wintertime.

> But the word of the Lord endureth for ever. And this is the word which by the gospel is preached unto you [1 Pet. 1:25].

My friend, we need the preaching and the teaching of the Word of God above everything else. I do not mean to minimize the place of music, the place of methods, and the place of organization, but there is absolutely no substitute for the Word of God today. "The word of the Lord endureth for ever."

CHAPTER 2

THEME: The suffering of the saints and the suffering of
Christ; suffering produces separation

THE SUFFERING OF THE SAINTS AND THE
SUFFERING OF CHRIST

In chapters 2—4 Peter deals with the suffering of God's children and
the suffering of the Lord Jesus Christ. And in these three chapters
we will see what suffering accomplishes in the lives of believers: Suffering produces separation (ch. 2); suffering produces Christian conduct (ch. 3); and suffering produces obedience to the will of God (ch.
4).

SUFFERING PRODUCES SEPARATION

In speaking of separation, or living for the Lord, there is the danger of
adopting one of two extreme viewpoints, both of which I consider very
much out of line with Scripture. One of them is thinking that human
nature is such that all it needs is merely new direction, it needs to be
given a purpose and a little reformation. The folk who take this position believe that since there is nothing wrong with human nature, they
need only to awaken the individual to his marvelous energy and intel-
lect and moral nature so that he will be able to live for the Lord. That is
one view of what it means to live the Christian life.

The second extreme viewpoint is that when one is born again, he
receives something that is supernatural (which he does receive), but
then he merely sits on the sidelines while God accomplishes in his life
all that needs to be done. Folk in this class become very pious. To me
they are like a puffed up frog. They never seem to grow and develop
into loving, full-orbed, normal Christians.

Now this second chapter will make it very clear that you and I,
through the New Birth (born again of incorruptible seed, the Word of

God), have a new nature, and we are to live in that new nature by the power of the Holy Spirit. We have been brought into a loving relationship with the one whom, having not seen, we love. Simon Peter saw Him and loved Him, and although you and I have not seen Him, the Holy Spirit can make Him real to us so that we love Him in that way also.

My friend, when you were first born again, do you remember how sweet and wonderful it was? Paul wrote to the Corinthian believers: "For I am jealous over you with godly jealousy: for I have espoused you to one husband, that I may present you as a chaste virgin to Christ" (2 Cor. 11:2). The Corinthian Christians had become very carnal. Their first love, that honeymoon love for Christ, was gone. God spoke of this same thing to His people Israel just before they went into the Babylonian captivity: ". . . Thus saith the LORD; I remember thee, the kindness of thy youth, the love of thine espousals, when thou wentest after me in the wilderness, in a land that was not sown" (Jer. 2:2). The children of Israel demonstrated that love when they first came out of Egypt and crossed the Red Sea. They sang a song of praises to Jehovah: ". . . I will sing unto the LORD, for he hath triumphed gloriously: the horse and his rider hath he thrown into the sea" (Exod. 15:1). Yet it wasn't too long before they became complainers before God. God remembers that.

My friend, today real separation rests upon the fact that you have been born again, you now have a new nature, and you are now in love with Christ. Your love for Him makes you want to please Him.

The great object in the purposes of God is to have folk saved, not only from judgment and the lake of fire, but saved from the present world. He wants them saved, not only for heaven by and by, but for the heart of Christ now. The work of Christ on the cross settled every question that sin has raised between God and our souls. The future is bright with the glory of God, and we have been brought into the value of that work of redemption. We have been born again, and no one—not even Satan—can change that.

However, my friend, how are we doing today in our Christian lives down here on the earth? How is our relationship with our fellow men and with the Lord Jesus Christ?

Wherefore laying aside all malice, and all guile, and hypocrisies, and envies, and all evil speakings,

As newborn babes, desire the sincere milk of the word, that ye may grow thereby [1 Pet. 2:1–2].

You see, we cannot expect God to do everything for us; He has certain things for us to do for ourselves. First, there are certain things that we are to lay aside. Paul, in his letter to the Ephesian believers, likens it to the taking off of a garment: "That ye put off concerning the former conversation the old man, which is corrupt according to the deceitful lusts. . . . Wherefore putting away lying, speak every man truth with his neighbour: for we are members one of another" (Eph. 4:22, 25).

Paul uses a different figure to describe this to the Corinthians. "Purge out therefore the old leaven, that ye may be a new lump, as ye are unleavened. For even Christ our passover is sacrifced for us: Therefore let us keep the feast, not with old leaven, neither with the leaven of malice and wickedness; but with the unleavened bread of sincerity and truth" (1 Cor. 5:7–8). When the Israelite observed the Passover and the Feast of Unleavened Bread, he didn't eat leavened bread; that is, he didn't go on living the same kind of life he had lived before. He was feeding in a different place on a different kind of bread. And it was a means of growth for him. Likewise, Paul is saying to the Corinthian believers that when they come to Christ, they are to get rid of the old leaven, which is symbolic of malice and wickedness in their lives. You see, we will never become perfect in this life, because we will always have that old nature.

"Laying aside all malice." What is malice? The best definition I have found is *congealed anger*. It means to have an unforgiving spirit. My friend, are you carrying bitterness in your heart and a chip on your shoulder? Although you witness about being born again and about loving Jesus, nobody around you will be able to distinguish that if you are carrying malice, congealed anger, in your heart.

"And all guile." Guile is using cleverness to get even or to try to make a good impression upon someone. Ananias and Sapphira used guile when they tried to represent themselves as being very generous givers to the church. That old nature which you and I have is good at that sort of thing. J. B. Lightfoot calls it "the vicious nature which is bent on doing harm to others."

"And hypocrisies, and envies, and all evil speakings." Hypocrisy is, of course, attempting to be what you are not. And evil speaking means slander.

"As newborn babes desire the sincere milk of the word." Instead of "sincere" milk, I translate it *pure* milk or *spiritual* milk. Just as a hungry baby reaches for the bottle, a believer is to desire the Word of God.

I remember when our little grandson was born. Because his father was over in Turkey at the time, his mother brought him into our home. We had him with us those first few months, and every now and then it was my task to give him his bottle. I want to tell you, that little fellow went into high gear when he saw that bottle of milk. He started moving his hands, his mouth, his feet—he was reaching out for it with every part of his body. At that time I was still the pastor of a congregation, and I thought, *I wish I had a congregation that would reach out after the Word of God like that!*

My friend, without a hunger for the Word of God you will not grow in grace and in the knowledge of Christ. You will not develop as a Christian—you will always be in your babyhood. We must remember that a little baby and a full-grown man are both human beings, but they are in different stages of growth and development. The little one needs milk so he can grow up to become a man. Now, how does a Christian grow? He grows by studying the Word of God. There is no growth apart from the Word of God.

I receive letters from many pastors who tell me that they are wet nurses for a lot of little babes. As one pastor said, "I spend my time burping spiritual babies!" Those babies should grow up so they wouldn't need a pastor to pat them and burp them all the time. And they would grow if they desired the pure milk of the Word.

It is my conviction that the "pure milk of the word" means the *total* Word of God. We don't grow spiritually by lifting out a verse for comfort here and there. We need the total Word of God to grow. We need a full, well-balanced diet. Of course, we start out with milk, but the day comes when we want a porterhouse steak, a good baked potato, a green salad, and maybe some black-eyed peas on the side. And you get all the spiritual nutrition you need in the total Word of God.

If so be ye have tasted that the Lord is gracious [1 Pet. 2:3].

"If so be" should be translated "since"—since ye have tasted that the Lord is gracious. You see, at the moment of salvation, a child is born with an appetite for the Word of God, just as a newborn infant immediately starts to eat. When my little grandson came home from the hospital at only two or three days old, all we had to do was stick a nipple in his mouth. He knew what to do. I didn't give him a lecture on how to drink milk; he seemed to know all about it. In the same way, I don't think we need programs to teach the spiritual babes in Christ how to get into the Word of God. Instead of *programs*, we need to give them the *Word* so they can feed on it.

What, then, is real separation? Real separation (we need to note this carefully) is a separation from the *works* of the flesh. Too many Christians feel that they must be separated from the world. No, we are *in* the world, and we must live in the world even though we are not *of* the world.

Let me give you an illustration about the wrong idea concerning separation. I drove an evangelist around Nashville, Tennessee, almost half of one night, trying to find a restaurant that didn't serve beer. This was his idea of separation from the world. We finally found one, and he got ptomaine poisoning from eating in that place! I wouldn't have eaten in it. I told him, "If I were you, after this I would go into a restaurant that serves good food and simply disregard the beer." You don't need to drink the beer just because you eat the food. Separation from the world does not mean that you cannot go into a restaurant that serves liquor.

Malice, hypocrisy, envy, evil speaking—these are the things from which we should be separated. Only the Spirit of God working within us will produce that kind of separation. And until you and I are willing to give up malice, hypocrisy, envy, and evil speaking, we will never grow to Christian maturity.

> To whom coming, as unto a living stone, disallowed in-
> deed of men, but chosen of God, and precious [1 Pet.
> 2:4].

"To whom coming as unto a living stone." We don't come to a little Babe in Bethlehem; we come as little babes to a living stone. The living stone is Christ. After the confession of Simon Peter, the Lord Jesus said, ". . . upon this rock I will build my church . . ." (Matt. 16:18). Simon Peter makes it very clear here that the living stone is not himself but that the living stone is Jesus Christ.

Jesus again refers to Himself as a stone in Matthew 21:42, 44: "Jesus saith unto them, Did ye never read in the scriptures, The stone which the builders rejected, the same is become the head of the corner: this is the Lord's doing, and it is marvellous in our eyes?" This is a quotation from Psalm 118. Now, speaking of Himself He says, "And whosoever shall fall on this stone shall be broken: but on whomsoever it shall fall, it will grind him to powder."

Christ Jesus is that foundation stone of the church. He is that stone today. Paul writes, "For other foundation can no man lay than that is laid, which is Jesus Christ" (1 Cor. 3:11). When you come as a sinner and fall on that stone, you are broken. However, in your brokenness that stone becomes a foundation for you, and that is your salvation. However, if you reject that stone, you are not through with the stone. Daniel, in his vision, saw a "stone was cut out without hands, which smote the image upon his feet" (see Dan. 2:34). That is the stone of judgment which will come to smite the earth. This stone symbolizes Christ. He also will be the stone of judgment to this earth. What a picture of the Lord Jesus is given to us here!

Here is something else that is wonderful—

> Ye also, as lively stones, are built up a spiritual house,
> an holy priesthood, to offer up spiritual sacrifices, ac-
> ceptable to God by Jesus Christ [1 Pet. 2:5].

"Ye also, as lively stones." Lively is an old English word for living. "Ye also, as living stones." How are we living stones? We have been "born again, not of corruptible seed, but of incorruptible, by the word of God, which liveth and abideth for ever" (v. 23, italics mine).

"Ye also, as living stones are built up a spiritual house." You will recall that after Peter's confession, "Thou art the Christ, the Son of the living God," the Lord Jesus said to him, "Thou art Peter and upon this rock I will build my church" (see Matt. 16:16, 18). The name *Peter* means "rock," and the Lord Jesus was saying to him in effect, "You are going to be a little stone, a pebble, but on this foundation stone [Christ] I am going to build My church." The Lord Jesus is the foundation stone, and we know that Peter understood it that way, because he said, "Ye also, as living stones, are built up a spiritual house." Just as Simon Peter was one of the little stones, you are one of the little stones and I am one of the little stones which are built into this spiritual house. When we are born again, become children of God, we are put into this building of God.

If we turn back to the Epistle to the Ephesians, we will find that Paul also uses this illustration of a building. "Now therefore ye are no more strangers and foreigners, but fellow-citizens with the saints, and of the household of God; And are built upon the foundation of the apostles and prophets, Jesus Christ himself being the chief corner stone; In whom all the building fitly framed together groweth unto an holy temple in the Lord: In whom ye also are builded together for an habitation of God through the Spirit" (Eph. 2:19–22). Today God is building a temple, a living temple. Those of us who come to Him as the sinners we are, who fall upon Him, cast ourselves upon Him for mercy, are saved. And He makes us a part of the living temple He is building upon the foundation stone, which is Christ Himself.

"An holy priesthood to offer up spiritual sacrifices, acceptable to God by Jesus Christ." Another picture which this epistle gives to us is that of a holy priesthood. All believers are living stones. All believers are priests. We are a holy priesthood, and later Peter calls it a royal priesthood. As priests we are to offer up spiritual sacrifices, acceptable to God in Jesus Christ. Praise to God is such a spiritual sacrifice. Your monetary offering to the Lord is such a spiritual sacrifice. I don't know why people think that money cannot be spiritual. It all depends on the way money is used. And then, you can offer yourself to God. That is a spiritual sacrifice.

> Wherefore also it is contained in the scripture, Behold, I lay in Sion a chief corner stone, elect, precious: and he that believeth on him shall not he confounded [1 Pet. 2:6].

This is a quotation from Isaiah 28:16: "Therefore thus saith the Lord God, Behold, I lay in Zion for a foundation a stone, a tried stone, a precious corner stone, a sure foundation: he that believeth shall not make haste." This stone is symbolic of Christ. Scripture makes this fact very clear.

> Unto you therefore which believe he is precious: but unto them which be disobedient, the stone which the builders disallowed, the same is made the head of the corner [1 Pet. 2:7].

"Unto you therefore which believe he is precious." A better translation would be, "For you therefore which believe is the preciousness." For you who believe there is the preciousness of Christ. I think it is so interesting that Simon Peter, the big, rugged fisherman, uses the word *precious*. We think of it as a word used in the vocabulary of women, but whenever Peter speaks of Christ or of His blood or any part about Him, he uses the word *precious*.

"But unto them which be disobedient, the stone which the builders disallowed [rejected], the same is made the head of the corner."

> And a stone of stumbling, and a rock of offence, even to them which stumble at the word, being disobedient: whereunto also they were appointed [1 Pet. 2:8].

This is a very important passage of Scripture. You will recall that it is a quotation from Psalm 118:22. There is a tradition that takes us back to the time of the building of Solomon's temple in Jerusalem. In 1 Kings 6:7 we read this about the actual construction of the temple: "And the house, when it was in building, was built of stone made ready before it was brought thither: so that there was neither hammer nor axe nor any tool of iron heard in the house, while it was in building." The stones, you see, were hewn to exact measurement in the quarry; and when they reached the building site, there was no sound of a hammer—they were just fitted into place.

Well, the tradition is that at the beginning of the project a very large, fine-looking stone came up from the quarry, but the builders couldn't fit it in any place; so they moved it to one side. Because it was in the way, eventually they just pushed it over the brow of the hill to make room for the other stones that they were receiving and forgot about it. Finally, when all the stones had been fitted into place, they sent down word to the quarry, "Send up the cornerstone." The building was finished except for the cornerstone. Word came back, "We sent the cornerstone to you at the very beginning." Then they remembered, "That's the stone we pushed off the hill!" So with a great deal of effort, they had to haul that stone back to the top of the hill, and they found that it did fit right into place. If this tradition is accurate, it certainly explains the verses before us.

The stone, which the builders rejected, has become the head of the corner. The stone is, of course, a picture of the Lord Jesus Christ. When He came into the world He was rejected by His own people—"He came unto his own, and his own received him not" (John 1:11). Not only then was He rejected, but you and I live today in a Christ-rejecting world. At the time this is being written, we are in the Christmas season. I don't know about your town, but in my town Christmas is being celebrated, but Jesus Christ is being rejected. About the most hypocritical thing in the world is to reject the one whose birthday you are celebrating! My friend, the Lord Jesus Christ is to you today either a stepping stone or a stumbling stone.

This brings us to a very wonderful passage of Scripture which reveals that a Christian's life is to be commensurate with his position in Christ. And until we live that life, we are not experiencing normal Christian living.

> But ye are a chosen generation, a royal priesthood, an holy nation, a peculiar people; that ye should shew forth the praises of him who hath called you out of darkness into his marvellous light [1 Pet. 2:9].

He is saying several very wonderful things about us here. We are a chosen generation, a royal priesthood, a holy nation, and a people of His own—not a "peculiar people." God's people are not supposed to be oddballs or crackpots or ready for the funny farm. Some folk seem to think that is what "peculiar" means. It is more meaningful to use the translation: *a people of His own.*

1. We are a "chosen generation," that is, an elect race. Back in the Old Testament God chose Israel as His people, and in the Scriptures there are two elect groups of people: the nation Israel, called an elect nation, and the church, called an elect nation and an elect people.

Now keep in mind that Peter is writing to his own people, the *Diaspora,* Jewish Christians who were scattered throughout the Roman Empire and even beyond it. In effect he is saying, "Although right now you certainly do not look like a chosen generation, an elect race, you are. Because you have come to Christ, you are a chosen generation, you are an elect nation, just as the children of Israel were elect. The keys of the kingdom have been given to the church, and we today are to give out the gospel because the church is the chosen instrument. This honor has been conferred upon believers. It is as if God had stamped out for you and me a wonderful medal on which is inscribed: You are an elect race; you are a chosen generation.

Many vain attempts are being made in our day to identify certain people of this earth with the ten "lost" tribes of Israel. They are said to be the gypsies, the Mormons, the Adventists, or the British-Israel group—which is probably the most vocal. Well, if they could prove that England and America were settled by the ten "lost" tribes of Israel, what have they proven? God has set aside the nation Israel temporarily, and today God is doing a new thing. He is calling out an elect race, a chosen generation, from every tongue and nation and people—both Jew and Gentile—and they are brought into a new relationship to God in the church.

Although you and I say that we have come to Christ, *He* says that He has chosen us. I like that. It reminds me of the story of two little urchins from the slums of New York who got to Macy's department store and were looking in the window at the merchandise on display. They saw things which they could never have, but they played a game with each other.

One said, "I choose this."

The other said, "I choose that."

The boy said, "I choose the ball."

The girl said, "I choose the doll."

You and I are just like poverty-stricken little urchins in this world, but when we say, "I choose Jesus," we find that He has already chosen us. How wonderful that is! The Lord Jesus said of His own apostles, "Ye have not chosen me, but I have chosen you . . ." (John 15:16). It is wonderful to know this. I am not being irreverent when I say that, since He has chosen me, He is responsible for me. The responsibility is His because I belong to Him. How wonderful it is that He has chosen us!

2. We are "a royal priesthood." Back in the Old Testament God first of all chose the entire nation of Israel to be His priests. (I believe that in the Millennium the whole nation of Israel will be priests here on this earth.) However, they sinned, and so God chose one tribe out of that nation. The priests came from this one tribe. Today there is no priesthood on earth which God recognizes—except one. Today every *believer* in the Lord Jesus Christ is a priest. Israel *had* a priesthood; today the church is a priesthood.

When I was a pastor, I preached a message entitled, "You Are a Catholic Priest." The word *catholic* means "general," of course. In that sense every believer is a catholic priest, and all have access to God. Since we belong to Christ, we can come into His presence, into the very holy of holies. Simon Peter tells us here that we as believers are members of a *royal* priesthood. We are children of the *King*. A little later on in this epistle we will read that the eyes of the Lord are over the righteous and that He *hears their prayers*. Oh, how wonderful this is!

3. We are "an holy nation." The nation Israel was never holy in conduct, and the same can be said of the church. Israel's failure is glaring;

the church's failure is appalling. Yet we are holy in our relationship with Him because Christ is our righteousness. If you have any standing before God, it is not in yourself; it is in Christ. I can't think of anything more wonderful than that today I stand complete in Him. What a joy it is to be a member of a holy nation, which is a new nation in the world today.

4. We are "a peculiar people"—a people of His own. We are a people for acquisition, a people for God's own possession. We belong to Him. Therefore, there is in the world not only a new nation but also a people that belong to Him. I don't know why some Christians are afraid of this concept. It doesn't mean that we are to be peculiar in conduct and act strangely but that we belong to Him. We are His very own people. We can compare it to a boy who goes out and gets a job and makes his own money for the first time. His dad has been giving him an allowance, but now the money belongs to him. It is something that he worked for, and it is his very own. Well, Christ's work, His work of redemption, required the shedding of His blood, as we have seen in this epistle, and now He has a people for His very own.

In the high priestly prayer of the Lord Jesus, He says, "I have manifested thy name unto the men which thou gavest me out of the world: thine they were, and thou gavest them me . . ." (John 17:6). Also He said, "All that the Father giveth me shall come to me; and him that cometh to me I will in no wise cast out" (John 6:37). How wonderful it is that the Father has given us to Christ!

And God calls His own. He calls you today, my friend. It doesn't matter who you are or to which race you belong. Jesus Christ is calling to you to be His own. He wants you to join a chosen generation and a royal priesthood. He is not inviting you to wear robes or to recite rituals but to join a priesthood that has access to God. He is asking you to belong to a new nation. He does not mean Germany or England or Japan or even the United States. He asks you to belong to that great company of believers out of every nation. " . . . happy is that people, whose God is the LORD" (Ps. 144:15). "So we [are] thy people and sheep of thy pasture . . ." (Ps. 79:13). Through the prophet Isaiah God says, ". . . for the transgression of my people was he stricken" (Isa. 53:8). And in the

New Testament, "Wherefore Jesus also, that he might sanctify the people with his own blood, suffered without the gate" (Heb. 13:12). Oh, what a wonderful position we have in Christ!

Which in time past were not a people, but are now the people of God: which had not obtained mercy, but now have obtained mercy [1 Pet. 2:10].

"Which in time past were not a people." We didn't belong to God but were far from Him.

"Which had not obtained mercy, but now have obtained mercy." My friend, there is one gift that you won't want to miss, and the name written on the box is "mercy." It is a big box because God is rich in mercy. If you need any today, you can go to Him for it.

Again, remember that Peter is writing specifically to the *Diaspora*, his people who were scattered abroad. "Which in time past were not a people"—they had rejected Christ as their Messiah and God had rejected them. "But are now the people of God." God was (and *is*) doing a new thing in calling out a people and extending His mercy to them.

Dearly beloved, I beseech you as strangers and pilgrims, abstain from fleshly lusts, which war against the soul [1 Pet. 2:11].

The child of God is to publish His praises. In what way? By singing hymns? Well, it is all right to do it that way, but you can better show forth His praises by not manifesting the works of the flesh. Earlier Peter has told us that the works of the flesh are malice, guile, hypocrisies, envies, and slander. We publish His praises by displaying our attitudes which have been shaped by the Word of God.

Having your conversation honest among the Gentiles: that, whereas they speak against you as evildoers, they may by your good works, which they shall behold, glorify God in the day of visitation [1 Pet. 2:12].

"Having your conversation [behavior] honest among the Gentiles." You see that true Christian separation is not some pious position that is to be assumed. It is not simply refraining from doing worldly things. It is very positive action. It includes honesty and good works. All believers in any kind of business dealing show forth the praises of God by their honesty. That is a witness to the world.

> **Submit yourselves to every ordinance of man for the Lord's sake: whether it be to the king, as supreme;**
>
> **Or unto governors, as unto them that are sent by him for the punishment of evildoers, and for the praise of them that do well [1 Pet. 2:13–14].**

Mad Nero was just coming to the throne in Rome as the new emperor. The Roman Empire boasted itself that it gave justice to man. However, it was like every other government, including our own. The poor man has never had a fair chance. The rich man has always been able to buy lawyers who were smart enough to evade the law. The poor man is the one who has the problems with the law.

Then what should be the believer's relationship to the law? He is to obey the law. That is what Peter is saying here—"submit yourselves to every ordinance of man for the Lord's sake." Since they were under Roman law, they were to obey it. Although Rome intended that their laws should be just, they were not. Remember that Roman law crucified Christ and persecuted the early Christians; yet Rome boasted loudly about justice. It sounds like modern America where religion—that is, the preaching of the Word of God—is very politely being suppressed. Are we to rebel against the government? No. We are to obey the laws of the land.

> **For so is the will of God, that with well-doing ye may put to silence the ignorance of foolish men [1 Pet. 2:15].**

When the Christian submits to government and to those who are in authority over his life, he is again revealing the praises of God through his life. I have never accepted joyfully a traffic ticket, but I pay my fine and try to be more careful to obey the laws. We are to be obedient to the law because we are giving a testimony.

> **As free, and not using your liberty for a cloak of maliciousness, but as the servants of God [1 Pet. 2:16].**

The relationship of the believer to other people is a testimony which speaks louder than the message from the pulpit. You see, the believer in Christ has a liberty which the man outside of Christ does not have. Believers have a marvelous liberty in Christ Jesus. I personally believe that I could go places and see things which the average Christian could not. Although I don't think I would be hurt by them, I avoid them because of my testimony. I don't want to use my liberty as a cloak of maliciousness; that is, I don't want my weaker brother to be hurt by what I do. We must remember that although we are *free*, we are the *servants* of God.

> **Honour all men. Love the brotherhood. Fear God. Honour the king [1 Pet. 2:17].**

"Honour all men." A Christian should respect other human beings. He doesn't say to *love* all men—believe me, some of them are very unlovely!

"Love the brotherhood." While we respect all men, we are to love the brotherhood, meaning other believers.

"Fear God." Certainly we as believers are to reveal by our lives that we are God-fearing people.

"Honour the king." We owe an honor to the office of the man who rules over us. I have never voted for a president whom I really wanted. I have always voted *against* the other candidate. I have never known a president who I felt was really capable. However, regardless of who is president and regardless of his inability, he should be honored because of his office. I am not impressed by some Scripture-spouting, pious individuals who attack the president of the United States. The office is to be honored.

Servants, be subject to your masters with all fear; not only to the good and gentle, but also to the froward [1 Pet. 2:18].

"Servants, be subject to your masters." In our contemporary culture we would say, "Employees, be subject to your bosses." Many folk tell me how wonderful it is to work for a Christian boss. But what if you are working for a godless fellow?

"Not only to the good and gentle, but also to the froward [perverse or unreasonable]." You are to be subject to him also, as long as he is not asking you to do that which is illegitimate or dishonest.

"Be subject" has in it the idea of freedom of choice. It is subjecting yourself, something you do voluntarily—not because you feel that your boss is a great person but because of your testimony for Christ. Christians also reveal the praise of God by their attitudes and actions in labor relationships.

For this is thankworthy, if a man for conscience toward God endure grief, suffering wrongfully.

For what glory is it, if, when ye be buffeted for your faults, ye shall take it patiently? but if, when ye do well, and suffer for it, ye take it patiently, this is acceptable with God [1 Pet. 2:19–20].

"For what glory is it if when ye be buffeted for your faults, ye shall take it patiently?" "Glory" could be translated "fame or praise." *Buffeted* means "to be struck with the fists." This was often the treatment of slaves in Peter's day. If a slave would steal or lie or become rebellious and refuse to work, his master might take him and give him a real going over with his fists. Peter is saying that if you have been beaten for any such fault, and you take it patiently, you have nothing to brag about. The beating was your own fault. God is not going to commend you for your patience in a case like that.

My friend, it may be possible that you are having problems and difficulties because you played the fool. A businessman said to me recently, "I have played the fool!" He had played the stock market and lost all his capital. He went bankrupt. When I was talking to him, he was suffering for his own foolishness. To recognize his fault and take the subsequent suffering patiently did not commend him to God.

"But if, when ye do well and suffer for it, ye take it patiently, this is acceptable with God." Of course, the natural reaction in all of us is to strike back when we have been unjustly treated. I confess that this is my first reaction, but I am learning to let God take care of it. God says in Romans 12:19, "Vengeance is mine; I will repay," and He does a much better job of it than I could. The Lord Jesus Himself said, "Blessed are ye, when men shall revile you, and persecute you, and shall say all manner of evil against you falsely, for my sake. Rejoice, and be exceeding glad: for great is your reward in heaven . . ." (Matt. 5:11–12). And Peter says, "This is acceptable with God."

Peter doesn't get very far without telling us about the Lord Jesus again, and here he reminds us of the sufferings of Christ, which are an example to us as believers.

> **For even hereunto were ye called: because Christ also suffered for us, leaving us an example, that ye should follow his steps:**
>
> **Who did no sin, neither was guile found in his mouth [1 Pet. 2:21–22].**

When our Lord Jesus Christ was here on earth, He suffered two kinds of suffering: He suffered as a human being down here when He became a man, suffering for righteousness' sake. Also, He suffered for the sins of the world.

Now, His suffering for the sins of the world is not an example for us—it is our redemption. It is something we believe and accept, but we can by no means imitate it. However, in His life down here He did leave us an example. In Nazareth during His first thirty years He suffered ridicule and misunderstanding, as Psalm 69 makes clear. Then, when He moved out in a public ministry, the gospel records tell us how He suffered for righteousness' sake. When you and I suffer for our faith, we remember the example He left for us in that connection.

> **Who, when he was reviled, reviled not again; when he suffered, he threatened not; but committed himself to him that judgeth righteously [1 Pet. 2:23].**

He let His Father settle the account. Again let me remind you of Romans 12:19: "Dearly beloved, avenge not yourselves, but rather give place unto wrath: for it is written, Vengeance is mine; I will repay, saith the Lord." Let's allow God to handle those accounts for us also. And He *will* handle them, by the way.

Jesus is suffering for the sins of the world in the next verse—

> **Who his own self bare our sins in his own body on the tree, that we, being dead to sins, should live unto righteousness: by whose stripes ye were healed [1 Pet. 2:24].**

This is not an *example* that is set for us. You and I cannot suffer to wash away our own sins, much less suffer for the sins of the world. Peter is talking here about redemption. "That we being dead to sins"— that was our condition.

"By whose stripes ye were healed." Healed of what? I notice that when so-called faith healers use the words, "by whose stripes ye were healed," they refer to Isaiah 53:5 rather than to this verse in 1 Peter, because Peter makes it evident that the healing is of *sins*. I certainly agree that the Lord Jesus came to be the Great Healer—but the Great Healer heals of sins. No human physician can handle that problem. And Peter's use of these words from Isaiah 53:5 reveals that the prophet Isaiah was not speaking primarily of physical healing but of that which is more important and more profound, healing from sin.

> **For ye were as sheep going astray; but are now returned unto the Shepherd and Bishop of your souls [1 Pet. 2:25].**

Humanity, both lost and saved, is called sheep. "Ye were as sheep going astray." This, too, is a quotation from Isaiah 53: "All we like sheep
have gone astray; we have turned every one to his own way; and the
LORD hath laid on him the iniquity of us all" (Isa. 53:6).

As you can see, the suffering of Christ is actually the theme of the
last part of this chapter. Christ suffered to set us an example, and He
suffered a vicarious, substitutionary death for our sins.

"But are now returned [the same word is often translated con-
verted] unto the Shepherd and Bishop [overseer] of your souls."

CHAPTER 3

THEME: Suffering produces Christian conduct in the home—in the church; Christ's suffering preached by the Spirit in Noah's day

In chapter 3 Peter teaches that suffering will also produce Christian conduct in the life of the believer. This conduct will be manifested in two different places, in the home and in the church.

CONDUCT IN THE HOME

Likewise, ye wives, be in subjection to your own husbands; that, if any obey not the word, they also may without the word be won by the conversation of the wives [1 Pet. 3:1].

"Likewise" means "in the same manner"; thus verse 1 ties right back into chapter 2 which discussed separation. "Conversation" would be better translated as "behavior." Separation and conduct are blended and molded together here.

In Ephesians 5 we find this same theme of the position of the wife in the home. However, Peter is presenting an altogether different situation from that which Paul discussed in Ephesians. Paul dealt with the relationship between a Christian wife and a Christian husband who were both *Spirit-filled* believers. That entire section in Ephesians begins with ". . . be filled with the Spirit" (Eph. 5:18). When you are filled with the Spirit, what are you to do? Paul says, "Wives, submit yourselves unto your own husbands, as unto the Lord" (Eph. 5:22), and "Husbands, love your wives, even as Christ also loved the church, and gave himself for it" (Eph. 5:25). He is speaking of a Christian home in which both the husband and wife are Spirit-filled believers, and the relationship is one in which the man loves his wife and is willing to die for her.

Now for the sake of order in any situation, there must be headship. In marriage, that headship has been given to the husband. When the wife is told to submit, however, it is not like the obedience of a child. Many men when they marry think of their wife as being a sort of first child and that she is to obey them like a child is to obey. That is not true at all. As we have suggested before, submission has to do with that which is voluntary. Paul is saying to the wife, "Submit yourself. This man loves you, and you are to submit to him." The better word, because it means more, is *respond*. Respond to this man. If he comes to you as your Christian husband and puts his arms around you and says, "I love you more than anything else," then certainly you should respond, "I love you."

Down through the years I have counseled a great many young people who have asked me to unite them in marriage. I never majored in trying to marry as many as I could; very frankly, I always did it with fear and trembling. I would like to mention very briefly some things I have told them.

Marriage is made on three different planes. The first is the physical plane, and that is important. It is the thing which the world talks about a great deal, the sexual relationship. It is a wonderful thing to have a wife whom you can put your arms around and love. Between two believers, sex can become the most precious, most beautiful, most wonderful thing there is in this world. It is my conviction that believers are the only ones who can really enjoy the physical relationship to the fullest. There is no question that the physical relationship is a wonderful thing.

When I got married, my wife felt she was not cut out to be a preacher's wife. She had been brought up in a little town in Texas and had seen how the preacher's wife was expected to do so much work in the church. I took her over to talk with Dr. Lewis Sperry Chafer one day, and I explained her fears to him. Neither of us will ever forget what Dr. Chafer said. He told my wife, "I am out speaking in Bible conferences a great deal. When I come home, I am not looking for an assistant pastor, I'm not looking for an organist, I'm not looking for a soloist, and I'm not looking for the president of the missionary society. I want a woman there to meet me who is my wife and whom I can put my arms around and love." The physical relationship is an important relationship.

The second plane in a marriage is the mental or psychological relationship, which is also very important. It is nice when the husband and wife enjoy doing the same things. On one of our tours to Bible lands, there was a very wonderful couple who were in their fifties. They would get up early in the morning and take a hike, and again at night they would walk together. They would visit certain places which were not included in the tour. They enjoyed doing things together, and it is wonderful to have that kind of relationship. The thing that makes the comic strip "Maggie and Jiggs" so funny is that Jiggs wants to go to Dinty Moore's where they have corned beef, cabbage, and beer, and Maggie wants to go to the opera where they have champagne. Their interests and their appetites are altogether different. That, of course, does not make for a healthy relationship. Because so many husbands and wives do not share the same interests, there are many clubs and lodges today where each can get away from the other and do what they want to do. How tragic that is!

The third plane in a marriage is the spiritual relationship, and this applies to a marriage between two believers. When problems and trouble and sorrow and suffering come, a husband and wife should be able to kneel down, come to God in prayer, and meet around the Word of God together. You can break the other two ties, but ". . . a threefold cord is not quickly broken" (Eccl. 4:12). When you have all three, you have a wonderful marriage. The first two cords can break, but if the third one will hold, the marriage will hold. However, when the third one is broken with the others, the marriage has gone down the tube, my friend. I have to admit it, there is very little hope for a marriage like that.

We have been discussing marriage between two believers. Suppose, however, that the wife is married to a man who is not a Christian. To begin with, she should not have married him, if that was the situation before they married. Any man or woman who marries a non-Christian is in trouble. Scripture forbids marriage between a believer and an unbeliever. In Deuteronomy we read, "Thou shalt not plow with an ox and an ass together" (Deut. 22:10). There are a lot of them yoked together today, and it is a big mistake.

One young lady came to me and said, "Dr. McGee, my fiancé is not a believer, but I am going to win him for the Lord." I said to her, "Have you won him yet?" "No," she said, "he won't even come to church with me yet." So I told her this: "Your greatest influence with that young man is right now. The day you get married, your influence to win him for the Lord will greatly diminish. You'll never be able to preach to him again. You are going to be living with him, and he's going to be watching you very carefully from now on. If you can't get him to church now, you're in trouble." She didn't like what I said. In fact, she went and got another preacher to perform the ceremony because I would not perform it. I do not marry—and have never knowingly married—a saved and an unsaved person; I believe that is entirely wrong. She got someone else to marry them, but she came back in two years weeping and wanting to talk to me because she had gotten a divorce from him. That marriage was headed in that direction even before it started, my friend.

In this passage here in 1 Peter, we have that unfortunate relationship in which there is a saved wife and an unsaved husband; apparently, the wife became a Christian after they had married. Is she to change after her conversion and become a sort of female preacher in the home in order to lecture her husband and to present the Gospel to him? No, she is to continue on in the same position of being in subjection to him. To be in subjection means to submit yourself. This is a voluntary step; it is not a command. The wife is to continue on in this relationship of voluntarily being in subjection, letting her husband—though unsaved—continue to be the head of the house.

Suppose, however, that her husband wants her to go with him to the nightclub and drink cocktails? Is she to do that? I would hope that even these most rabid folk who say that she should obey her husband would agree that she should not do such things. However, there are those who are giving that kind of counsel today.

A lady who attended my church when I was a pastor in downtown Los Angeles had an unsaved husband who wanted her to go to a nightclub, which apparently was a sort of burlesque. Some evangelist had counseled her that she was to obey her husband even in this, and so she went. It offended her sensibilities, and she was under great conviction about it. She actually came to the place where a doctor told her that she would have to enter an institution for psychopathic treatment because she could not go on under that type of pressure. Well, she heard me speaking on the radio, and it was evident that I had a little different idea about it. When she came to talk to me, I told her that I did not believe that Simon Peter intended for her to do these things. I said that after her conversion she was to try to win her husband and to be subject to him. But I went on to ask her what she would do if her husband wanted her to go out and commit a robbery. Would she have to join him in that and drive the car for him? She said she was sure that the evangelist would not want her to go that far.

May I say to you, her submission was to be voluntary. God certainly did not command her to engage in sinful or questionable activities which would spoil her testimony. A Christian wife must live very carefully before an unsaved husband. Her preaching is not going to do a bit of good. "That, if any obey not the word, they also may without the word be won by the behavior of the wives." In other words, she is to preach a wordless sermon by her pure life which she lives before him. And that has nothing in the world to do with submission to him.

While they behold your chaste conversation coupled with fear [1 Pet. 3:2].

Peter says that your husband will recognize that you have now changed and want to live a pure life for God and that you no longer want to indulge in the things of the world. Therefore, that is the testimony which you can give to him.

Another lady came to me when I was a pastor and said, "Dr. McGee, I bring my husband to church every Sunday." (She was the kind of woman who *could* bring her husband; she was a dominant personality.) She continued, "He is not saved, and every Sunday I think he will make a decision for Christ but he doesn't. On Monday morning I sit at the breakfast table just weeping and telling him how I wish he would accept Christ. When he comes home from work in the evening, again I just sit there at dinner and weep and beg him to accept Christ." I got to thinking about what she had said. How would you like to have dinner every evening and breakfast every morning with a weeping woman? I wouldn't care for it myself, and I'm sure you wouldn't want that either. So I called her up and said, "Suppose that for a year's moratorium you simply do not talk to your husband about the Lord at all?" She said, "Oh, you mean that I'm not to witness?" I said, "No, I didn't say that. Peter says that if you cannot win your husband with the Word, then start preaching a wordless sermon. How about your life? What kind of life are you living before him?" I want to tell you, that put her back on her heels because she wasn't living as she knew she should live. But she agreed to my suggestion because she did want to win him, and she was a wonderful woman in many ways. I was amazed myself when, in six months' time, her husband made a decision for Christ one Sunday morning. The wordless sermon had won, my friend.

> **Whose adorning let it not be that outward adorning of plaiting the hair, and of wearing of gold, or of putting on of apparel [1 Pet. 3:3].**

Obviously, this verse does not prohibit all adorning—if it did, it also would prohibit all apparel!

In the Roman Empire a great emphasis was put upon the way women arranged their hair. If you have seen any pictures of that period, you know that the women loaded their heads down with all kinds of hair, not their own hair but someone else's. They really built their hair up, and they wore jewelry in it. Today we have very much the same kind of emphasis upon hair and dress. If the unsaved man you are going to marry cannot be won to Christ by your sex appeal before you marry, you will never win him to Christ by sex appeal afterward. A wife can apply a gallon of perfume and wear the thinnest negligee there is, but I tell you, she will not win him for the Lord that way.

I do believe, though, that a Christian woman should dress in style.

At the Bible institute where I used to teach, someone had given the girls the notion that they should never use any makeup and need not give any care to the way they dressed. I used to tell those girls that we all ought to look the best we can with what we've got to work with, although some of us don't have much to work with! I said, "Some of you would look a little bit better if you would put on just a little makeup, because you look like you came out of the morgue. That is simply not attractive, and it does not commend you to God."

Peter's point here is that you cannot win an unsaved man by sex appeal.

> But let it be the hidden man of the heart, in that which is not corruptible, even the ornament of a meek and quiet spirit, which is in the sight of God of great price [1 Pet. 3:4].

A woman is to wear an ornament, but it is to be an ornament on the inside, the ornament of a gentle and quiet spirit. In the little Book of Ruth, we read that when Boaz went into the field and saw that beautiful maid of Moab, Ruth, he fell in love with her. But have you noticed something else? Boaz had heard of her character. He had heard that she had a marvelous, wonderful character, and he fell in love with her total person.

We have many very helpful cosmetic products today, and I see nothing wrong in using anything that will make you look better. All of us want to look the best we possibly can. Alexander Pope has well advised:

> Be not the first by whom the new are tried,
> Nor yet the last to lay the old aside.

Be in style. Dress up in a way that is becoming, but don't try to use that as the means of winning someone to the Lord. We need more inward adornment today—that is the thing which is important.

> For after this manner in the old time the holy women
> also, who trusted in God, adorned themselves, being in
> subjection onto their own husbands [1 Pet. 3:5].

There are a number of fine examples of such women in the Old Testament. I have already mentioned Ruth who was in the genealogical line that led to Christ. We are also told that Rachel was a beautiful woman, and Jacob fell in love with her. She was the one bright spot in that man's life, which was a pretty dark life, by the way.

> Even as Sara obeyed Abraham, calling him lord: whose
> daughters ye are, as long as ye do well, and are not
> afraid with any amazement [1 Pet. 3:6].

Sarah was such a beautiful woman that several kings wanted her as a wife, and Abraham had a great problem in that connection. But she called Abraham "lord." She looked up to Abraham. It is wonderful when a wife can look up to her husband.

Now Peter speaks to the husbands—

> Likewise, ye husbands, dwell with them according to
> knowledge, giving honour unto the wife, as unto the
> weaker vessel, and as being heirs together of the grace
> of life; that your prayers be not hindered [1 Pet. 3:7].

Although this seems to imply that both the husband and wife are Christians, I believe that these instructions to husbands would be applicable either way.

A husband is to treat his wife as the weaker vessel, and he is to give her honor because of that. I do not think the current women's liberation movement is going to last very long. I think a woman wants to be a woman, just as a man wants to be a man. Because she is the weaker vessel, she is to be treated with honor. The man is to give first place to her. She gets into the car first as he holds the door for her. When they enter a room, she goes first. As they walk down the sidewalk, he walks on the outside for her protection. He is to treat her with honor. When a woman loses her place, she doesn't go up; she goes down. When she takes her place, she can be treated with honor and given her rightful position. I think every husband ought to treat his wife as someone special.

"That your prayers be not hindered." Peter says that if you are not getting along as husband and wife, it will ruin your family altar, and there is no use praying together. If you are fighting like cats and dogs, well, God just doesn't hear cats and dogs. But when you are in agreement, you can pray together and your prayers will not be hindered.

Before we leave this particular section of Scripture, I would like to add one further word. Marriage is something which God has given to the entire human family, not only to Christians or to the nation Israel. In the Book of Genesis we are told that God made man, and at that time man was alone. I think the Lord let Adam be alone for a long time to let him know he was missing something. Then Scripture says that God took man and from man He made woman. Using the Hebrew words, Genesis 2:23 reads, "She shall be called Isha, because she was taken out of Ish." She is called ". . . an help meet for him" (Gen. 2:18, italics mine); that is, a help that was fit for him. In other words, she was to be the other half of him. He was only half a man, and she was to be the other part of him. With that in mind, you can see that the marriage relationship is not to be one of a man insisting on treating his wife like a little child who has to jump every time he says so. She is there to help him. She is there to be a part of him. She is there to love him. And he is there to love and protect her. That is the ideal relationship in marriage.

CONDUCT IN THE CHURCH

Finally, be ye all of one mind, having compassion one of another, love as brethren, be pitiful, be courteous [1 Pet. 3:8].

Believers are to be like-minded, sympathetic, tenderhearted, and courteous, which means they are to be humble-minded, not trying to lord it over one another. This is to be the attitude and action of a believer among other believers.

> Not rendering evil for evil, or railing for railing: but
> contrariwise blessing; knowing that ye are thereunto
> called, that ye should inherit a blessing [1 Pet. 3:9].

This is turning the other cheek. If another believer says something evil about you, something that is not true, are you to strike back? No. Commit him to the Lord—the Lord will take care of him. If we take this position it will break down all the little cliques and stop all the fighting within the church. Remember that we are representing the Lord.

> For he that will love life, and see good days, let him re-
> frain his tongue from evil, and his lips that they speak
> no guile [1 Pet. 3:10].

All of us want to live, but unfortunately there are a lot of believers today who are not enjoying life. They are not living life to its fullest, not getting all they should out of life. When I was a pastor in Nashville, Tennessee, many years ago, a young medical student—who was the president of the young people's group in the church and not much younger than I was—said one day, "Vernon, I want life to be like an orange to me, an orange out of which I can squeeze every drop. I want to live for God!" "For he that will love life"—if you want to really live, here is a good formula, and here is the key to it. Peter says that we are to refrain from constantly speaking evil of others. And we are to refrain from speaking "guile," from being deceptive and not telling the truth.

> Let him eschew evil, and do good; let him seek peace,
> and ensue it [1 Pet. 3:11].

A child of God is not to sit back and act piously. Let's live it up, my friend, but let's not live it up by indulging in gossip and evil. Let's live it up by turning away from evil and pursuing that which ministers to peace. Let's live for God today. How important this is!

**For the eyes of the Lord are over the righteous, and his
ears are open unto their prayers: but the face of the Lord
is against them that do evil [1 Pet. 3:12].**

This is an amazing passage of Scripture. Peter is quoting here from
Psalm 34: "The eyes of the LORD are upon the righteous, and his ears
are open unto their cry. The face of the LORD is against them that do
evil, to cut off the remembrance of them from the earth" (Ps.
34:15–16). This is a strong statement as it is given here in this psalm.
It is something the Word of God has emphasized a great deal. God has
guaranteed to hear the prayers of those who are His own. He has not
guaranteed to hear the prayers of those who are not His own. The only
prayer that a sinner can pray is, "Lord, I admit that I am a sinner, and
accept Jesus Christ as my Savior, and ask that You accept me in Him."
That is a prayer that God will hear and that God will answer. Many
people today have the idea that an old reprobate can live any kind of
life he wants and then come to God in prayer when he is in trouble and
expect God to hear and answer him. As the movies and the novels tell
it, the old reprobate comes home to find his little girl sick in the hospital, and so he gets down on his knees and calls upon God to raise her
up. How sentimental that is! May I say this very plainly: it is nonsense,
and it is absolutely unscriptural. Let that old reprobate get right with
God, and then God will hear and answer his prayer. It is a false idea
today to think that you can call on God under any circumstances
whether or not you are His child. My friend, He has not promised to
hear the prayers of those who are not His own.

In Ecclesiastes 2:17 we read the statement of a man who has tried
everything in life. He has lived like a reprobate, and he says, "Therefore I hated life: because the work that is wrought under the sun is
grievous unto me: for all is vanity and vexation of spirit." How many
men and women today who are involved in living for the things of this
world suddenly wake up and find that it's not worth it? Life is monoto-
nous, and life is not worth it. No wonder they put a gun to their heads
and blow their brains out. No wonder some of them jump off bridges.
No wonder some take an overdose of sleeping pills. My friend, it is not

until you come into a right relationship with God that you can live life to its fullest.

Does that mean that a child of God is living on a pretty high plane above the problems of this world? Listen to Peter—

> **And who is he that will harm you, if ye be followers of that which is good? [1 Pet. 3:13].**

Does that mean that God gives you an armor so that nobody can touch you at all?

> **But and if ye suffer for righteousness' sake, happy are ye: and be not afraid of their terror, neither be troubled [1 Pet. 3:14].**

Suffering for the right should bring joy to the child of God. Some Christians actually make themselves obnoxious in their witness to others, thinking they are taking a stand for the Lord. But if we have simply taken a quiet stand for the right and for God, we ought to rejoice if we suffer for that. I must repeat this again: you are not going to escape suffering in this world if you are a child of God. Someone has said, "Jesus often spoke of Christianity as a banquet but never as a picnic." How true that is! He never said that we are going to have it easy down here.

I truly wish that I could elucidate this next verse in such a way that it would bless your heart. I will do my best.

> **But sanctify the Lord God in your hearts: and be ready always to give an answer to every man that asketh you a reason of the hope that is in you with meekness and fear [1 Pet. 3:15].**

This means you ought to know more than a little about the Bible. The tragedy of the hour is that there are so many folk who say they are Christians, but the sceptic is able to tie them up into fourteen different knots like a little kitty caught up in a ball of yarn—they cannot extricate themselves at all. Why? Because of the fact that they do not know the Word of God. "Sanctify the Lord God in your hearts." Oh, today, do you have a little sanctuary, a little chapel in your own heart? When you are riding along in the car or walking down the street or are in the shop or office or classroom,is there a little chapel in your heart where you can withdraw and sanctify the Lord God in your heart? If there is, folk outside will know that you belong to God, and you will not have to mouth it all the time or make yourself obnoxious by making some pious statement. Oh, if in our lives today we would sanctify the Lord God in our hearts. How we need to do that!

Habakkuk wrote, "But the LORD is in his holy temple: let all the earth keep silence before him" (Hab.2:20). On Sunday you may go to your church, but the world is passing you by, headed for the beach, headed for the mountains, headed for the desert, headed for places of amusement. The whole world is not keeping silence before Him. Why? Because we as individuals need to sanctify the Lord God in our hearts.

Having a good conscience; that, whereas they speak evil of you, as of evildoers, they may be ashamed that falsely accuse your good conversation in Christ [1 Pet. 3:16].

In other words, make sure that those who speak evil of you are in error. Shortly after I had come to downtown Los Angeles as pastor of a church there, I met Dr. Jim McGinley in Chicago at the Moody Founder's Week conference, and he asked me, "How do you like being pastor of that great church?" I said, "It's wonderful, but I find myself in a place where I cannot really defend myself. I don't intend to get up in the pulpit every Sunday morning to explain all the things that have been said about me. My business is teaching the Word of God. Yet none of the things that have been said are true." Dr. McGinley said to me, "Just thank the Lord that what they say is not true." In this verse Peter is saying, "Have a good conscience so that when you hear these rumors about yourself, it will not bother you because you know they are not true."

> For it is better, if the will of God be so, that ye suffer for
> well doing, than for evil doing [1 Pet. 3:17].

If you suffer for Christ's sake, you can rejoice in that; but if you are suffering because you have played the fool, because you have gotten into trouble and into sin, then that is a different story altogether.

CHRIST'S SUFFERING PREACHED BY THE SPIRIT IN NOAH'S DAY

> For Christ also hath once suffered for sins, the just for
> the unjust, that he might bring us to God, being put to
> death in the flesh, but quickened by the Spirit [1 Pet.
> 3:18].

It is important for us to see that Jesus Christ became a human being, and it was in His humanity that He died on the cross. He *died* on the cross, and it was the Holy Spirit who raised Him from the dead.

> By which also he went and preached unto the spirits in
> prison [1 Pet. 3:19].

This has been a most misunderstood passage of Scripture. The key word to this entire passage is in verse 20; it is the little word *when*—

> Which sometime were disobedient, when once the
> longsuffering of God waited in the days of Noah, while
> the ark was a-preparing, wherein few, that is, eight
> souls were saved by water [1 Pet. 3:20].

When did Christ preach to the spirits in prison? "When once the longsuffering of God waited in the days of Noah." In Christ's day, the spirits of those men to whom Noah had preached were in prison, for they had rejected the message of Noah. They had gone into *sheol*. They were waiting for judgment; they were lost. But Christ did not go down and preach to them after He died on the cross. He preached through

Noah "when once the longsuffering of God waited in the days of Noah." For 120 years Noah had preached the Word of God. He saved his family but no one else. It was the Spirit of Christ who spoke through Noah in Noah's day. In Christ's day, those who rejected Noah's message were in prison. The thought is that Christ's death meant nothing to them just as it means nothing to a great many people today who, as a result, will also come into judgment.

The like figure whereunto even baptism doth also now save us (not the putting away of the filth of the flesh, but the answer of a good conscience toward God,) by the resurrection of Jesus Christ [1 Pet. 3:21].

"The like figure whereunto even baptism doth also now save us." To what baptism does this refer? It is not water baptism but the baptism of the Holy Spirit. The baptism of the Holy Spirit is real baptism, and water baptism is ritual baptism. Now I believe in water baptism, and I believe immersion is the proper mode. However, the important thing here is to see that it is the baptism of the Holy Spirit which puts you into the body of believers.

"Not the putting away of the filth of the flesh"—it is not just by water, for that will not put away the filth of the flesh. "But the answer of a good conscience toward God, by the resurrection of Jesus Christ"—that is, a faith in the resurrection of Jesus Christ which brought the work of the Holy Spirit into your life and regenerated you.

Who is gone into heaven, and is on the right hand of God; angels and authorities and powers being made subject unto him [1 Pet. 3:22].

This verse is speaking of the Lord Jesus Christ. You and I are little sinners down here, but we can come to Him, receive Him, and thus join the great company of the redeemed. We are baptized by the Holy Spirit into the body of Christ because He is raised from the dead and is today at God's right hand.

CHAPTER 4

THEME: Suffering produces obedience to the will of God

SUFFERING PRODUCES OBEDIENCE TO THE WILL OF GOD

In this passage of Scripture Peter makes it very clear that when life is easy there is danger of drifting into a state of mind which accepts every blessing in life as if it were owed to us. We come to the place where we do not prize or value life as we should. As a Christian, what value do you put upon life? God permits His children to suffer in order to keep us from sin and to give us a proper value of life. I hear so many young people today say that they did this or that in order to find a new direction for their life. May I say to you, suffering will give a new direction to life. David discovered this and wrote in Psalm 66:10, "For thou, O God, hast proved us: thou hast tried us, as silver is tried." God puts us through the test that it might draw us to Himself and give us a new direction and drive for life. Such is the purpose of suffering.

> **Forasmuch then as Christ hath suffered for us in the flesh, arm yourselves likewise with the same mind: for he that hath suffered in the flesh hath ceased from sin [1 Pet. 4:1].**

I must confess that I have recently been given new insights into this verse. Over the years it is a verse that has disturbed me a great deal, and I have never gone into a great deal of detail in my teaching on it. I have been rather amazed to discover that other commentators have likewise more or less bypassed it rather than dealing with it in detail. I trust that the Spirit of God will give us an understanding that will make this verse helpful to us.

"Forasmuch" refers us back, I believe, to 1 Peter 3:18, "For Christ also hath once suffered for sins, the just for the unjust, that he might bring us to God, being put to death in the flesh, but quickened by the Spirit." These two verses go together, and this is again a reminder that in His human body Christ not only endured pain but He was actually put to death in the flesh.

In recent years there was a very popular book, *When God Died*, as well as a popular theology which said, "God is dead." Well, God never died, my friend, and He is not dead today—He hasn't even been sick. Christ died in His human body, which He took yonder at Bethlehem. As the writer to the Hebrews put it, He was "in all points tempted like as we are." He knew what it was to suffer. He knew what it was to bleed. He knew what it was to shed tears. He knew what it was to be brokenhearted. He was perfectly human, and He died in that human body.

Christ brought an end to His relation to the sins of man when He died on the cross because He bore the penalty for sin in His own body. We are told back in 1 Peter 2:24, "Who his own self bare our sins in his own body on the tree, that we, being dead to sins, should live unto righteousness: by whose stripes ye were healed." Three times (1 Pet. 2:24; 3:18; 4:1) Peter says that it was in His flesh and in His body that Christ paid the penalty for man's sin. That leads me to say this: Christ did not die *in* sin, nor did He die *under* sin, but He died *to* sin. He took my place, He took your place, and He paid the penalty for our sin. From that point on, Christ will not come back to die for sin. He will no longer have any relationship to sin Himself because of the fact that He arose from the dead. When He came back from the dead, He came in a glorified body. He was "quickened by the Spirit," or "made alive by the Spirit" is the better translation (see 1 Pet. 3:18). He has a life that now lives in a body. He is up yonder in a body that is completely devoted to the service of God, for He is God, and He is in the enjoyment of full and free access to God and to all creation.

Now Christ is able to make over this benefit to us. Peter tells us, "Arm yourselves likewise with the same mind." "The same *mind*" actually means "the same *thought*." Some people have said that it means *resolution*, but that is not quite the idea. This refers to the *thought* which leads to a resolution. This is what Paul spoke of when he said, "Let this mind be in you, which was also in Christ Jesus" (Phil. 2:5).

"Christ hath suffered for us in the flesh," Peter says, and those of us who have suffered in the flesh have "ceased from sin." The translation of the word *ceased* is a very unsatisfactory one, and this is what had disturbed me about this verse. The Greek word translated as "ceased" is *pauō*. In the active voice, *pauō* means "to stop or to cease." It is used like that in 1 Corinthians 13:8, "Whether there be tongues, they shall cease"; that is, tongues are going to stop, and that is something I have emphasized in my teaching. When I was in Athens, Greece, I took a walk from the Hilton Hotel down to Constitution Square. As I would come to a corner, I would see a sign like our "Stop" sign, only there it said, *Pauō. Pauō* means "to stop" when it is used in the active voice. An active verb means that the subject does something; a passive verb (or the middle voice in the Greek) means that the subject is acted upon and the subject itself doesn't do anything. In this verse which we are studying, *pauō* is in the middle voice or the passive. Therefore Dr. Joseph Thayer, in his lexicon of the New Testament, translates this literally as "hath got release." In other words if you have suffered in the flesh, you've got release from sin. Just what does Peter mean by this? First of all, I would say that God will use suffering to keep you from sin. I am confident that many of us have experienced that personally. Suffering will keep us from sin, but Peter is saying more than that here. Peter says we have got *release* from sin. That means that God has made an adequate provision for you and me to live the Christian life. Dr. Griffith Thomas has said that in this verse Peter puts Paul's Romans 6 into a nutshell of just one verse. Romans 6 is that chapter which speaks of the provision God has made for you and me to live the Christian life.

Peter has made it very clear that we have been born again by the Word of God. The Spirit of God using the Word of God will produce a son of God. And that son of God now has a new nature, a new nature that is *not* going to live in sin.

The Bible's illustration of this truth, which I use a great deal, is the story of the Prodigal Son (see Luke 15:11-32). The Prodigal Son got down in the pigpen, but, you see, he wasn't a pig. He had the nature of his father who lived down the road in that wonderful mansion. Because that boy had the nature of his father, he didn't like eating out of a trough. He didn't like eating the swill that the swine ate. He enjoyed sitting down at a table covered with a white linen tablecloth and eating with a knife and fork. He liked having a nice steak or prime rib before him, with all the other delicacies, topped off with ice cream. That boy didn't care for the pigpen for he had the nature of his father.

Peter says you are now identified with Christ. When you came to the Lord Jesus and were born again, the Spirit of God baptized you, that is, He identified you with Christ. Now let that mind, that thought, be in you which is in Christ. Christ is up yonder at God's right hand in a body totally devoted to the service of God for you and me. Do you think, my friend, if you have really been born again, if you are really a child of God with a new nature, that you can go on living in sin? Now I am a Calvinist and I emphasize the security of the believer. However, I think that there is such an overemphasis on that point that many of our Arminian friends also need to be heard today. This is one reason I feel as kindly as I do toward the Pentecostals; they are preaching a doctrine that has been largely forgotten, the doctrine of holiness. They emphasize that believers should live a holy life for God today. My friend, you *cannot* be a child of God and go out and live in the pigpen. Let's face it—if you do, you are a pig. Pigs live in pigpens and they love it, but sons do not love the pigpen.

Peter says that God has made every provision for you: you are born again, indwelt by the Spirit, baptized by the Spirit, identified with Christ, and you can now live life by the power of the Spirit of God. In Romans 7 Paul shows how the Christian is defeated when he lives in the flesh, but in Romans 8 he tells how God has provided the Holy Spirit that we might live by the power of the Spirit. Again I come back to this word *pauō*. It is not used in the active voice; what we have here is a word that does not mean "cease," but means "hath got release." God has made every arrangement for you and me not to live in sin today. It would be impossible for us to live in sin. Oh, the son might go to the pigpen, but you can put this down for sure, he will not *stay* in the pigpen. One day he has to say, "I will arise and go to my father . . ." (Luke 15:18).

If you are living in sin today and you are comfortable in it, I would surely question your salvation. Someone may ask, "Can a Christian do this or do that?" He might do it one time, my friend, but if he lives in sin there is something radically wrong. A child of God with a new nature longs to please Christ in all things. This is the reason that I believe the study of the entire Word of God is essential today. I know that I will be accused of playing on an instrument of only one string. Well, since I'm no musician, I have an instrument with only one string on it, and it is this: You need the *total* Word of God—not just a few little verses to draw out some little legalistic system by which to live the Christian life. You cannot live the Christian life by following rules. You can live the Christian life only by having the mind of Christ, by having the Spirit of God moving in you to please God and to refrain from those things which bring disgrace to Him.

That he no longer should live the rest of his time in the flesh to the lusts of men, but to the will of God [1 Pet. 4:2].

Paul speaks very strongly in this connection in Romans 8: "For they that are after the flesh do mind the things of the flesh; but they that are after the Spirit the things of the Spirit. For to be carnally minded is death; but to be spiritually minded is life and peace" (Rom. 8:5-6). What does Paul mean when he says "to be carnally minded is death"? Do you lose your salvation? No, it means you are dead to any fellowship with God. "If we say that we have fellowship with him, and walk in darkness, we lie, and do not the truth" (1 John 1:6). My friend, you *cannot* live in sin and have fellowship with God. Sin is what is keeping people away from the Word of God today. I have to confess that Christians are a minority, and in teaching through the entire Bible as I do, I appeal only to the minority of the minority. A great many folk are trying to find a shortcut to living the Christian life, and there is no shortcut. God says that He will use suffering in your life in order to keep you from sin.

"That he no longer should live the rest of his time in the flesh to the lusts of men, but to the will of God." We no longer take life for granted, for we have suffered, and God will use that suffering to keep us from sin.

As he continues, Peter begins to look ahead. Life is short—

For the time past of our life may suffice us to have wrought the will of the Gentiles, when we walked in lasciviousness, lusts, excess of wine, revellings, banquetings, and abominable idolatries [1 Pet. 4:3].

After we have been converted, we would be very foolish to spend our lives in the things which we did before. In fact, we cannot do that. We are now joined to Christ; we are united to Him, and we cannot run with the world to sinning. We must live today for God. What a tremendous truth this is! Life is short; time is fleeting, and we must recognize that we are going to come before Him for judgment before long.

"When we walked in lasciviousness, lusts, excess of wine, revellings, banquetings, and abominable idolatries." Simon Peter spells out the sins here. Homer Rodeheaver was a personal friend of mine, and I loved him in the Lord. Years ago as we were having lunch together, I said to him, "Homer, you were with Billy Sunday for so many years. What do you say was the secret of his ministry?" He replied, "He preached on sin, and he always was specific when he spoke about sin. He spelled it out." Simon Peter spells it out here.

"Lasciviousness"—that's living in sexual sin. "Lusts"—that includes a great many things, lusting after the things of the flesh. "Excess of wine" is drunkenness. "Revellings, banquetings, and abominable idolatries." "Banquetings" should be translated "carousing." "Abominable idolatries"—the Scriptures tell us that the love of money is the root of all evil; covetousness is idolatry in our day. These are the things which will take you away from God, and Peter clearly spells them out.

I am afraid that today we have a great many preachers who are pretty indefinite about sin. Some wag wrote: "If you've got religion, you don't know it. If you know it, you haven't got it. And if you've got it, you can't lose it. And if you lose it, you didn't have it. And if you never had it, you can't get it." Some of the talk I hear today sounds as

vague as that. My friend, sin is spelled out here. It is written in bold
letters; it's in neon lights in the Word of God, and there is no way of
missing it.

> **Wherein they think it strange that ye run not with them
> to the same excess of riot, speaking evil of you [1 Pet.
> 4:4].**

Either you are going to please God or you'll please men. And if you are
pleasing men, you will not please God. The Lord Jesus said, "If the
world hate you, ye know that it hated me before it hated you" (John
15:18). If the world does not hate you, then there is something radically wrong.

When I was sixteen years old, I began to work in a bank. They put
me on the teller's cage when I was seventeen and promised me that the
next year I would be made a junior officer. I felt that I was well liked
and popular in that bank. Then I went to a young people's conference
where I made my decision for Christ and to study for the ministry. I
came back to the bank and resigned, yet they let me have a part-time
job—they were good to me in that way. But I found out that I was no
longer the popular boy in that place. As a Christian I became very
unpopular. In fact, the fellows with whom I had run ridiculed me, and
they did a good job of it because they knew what my life had been
before. That was a very difficult decision I made at that particular
time.

I hope that I am not misunderstood when I tell this little story. In
those days I went to dances; in fact, I was chairman of a dance commit-
tee. After I made my decision for Christ, I thought I would break off my
old ties gradually. I went to the next dance with the idea that I would
not dance but I would just stand around in the stag line. As I was
standing there, I felt very much out of place. There was a fellow there
from the bank above whom I had been promoted. He didn't care much
for me, especially when I announced that I was studying for the
ministry—yet he was an officer in a church himself. He came over to
me at that dance and said, "This is a h—— of a place for a preacher
to be!" Do you know, that was the first time he had ever told me the

truth. I agreed with him. I found out that you cannot break off gradually. The world is not going to appreciate you very much when as a
Christian you try to continue on with them. I walked out of that place,
never to walk back in again.

My friend, I do not believe that you can go on in sin if you are a
child of God. You have the nature of Christ; you are joined to Him. He
suffered down here once; He is suffering no more, but He can help you.
He sent the Holy Spirit down to indwell those who are His own. We
have been baptized into the body of believers, as Peter has pointed out
to us, and now, being filled with the Holy Spirit, we can live for God.
We cannot do it in our own strength but in His strength.

> **Who shall give account to him that is ready to judge the
> quick and the dead [1 Pet. 4:5].**

"Ready to judge the quick [the living] and the dead." The whole world,
the living and the dead, are going to be judged by the Lord Jesus someday. Will He judge believers, too? He sure will! Not for salvation,
which was assured when they became children of God, but He will not
let a believer get by with sin since He is judging the world for sin.
Because God does judge Christians in the world—He chastens His
children—the unbeliever had better beware. He is warned that he will
come up someday for judgment.

> **For for this cause was the gospel preached also to them
> that are dead, that they might be judged according to
> men in the flesh, but live according to God in the spirit.
> [1 Pet. 4:6].**

"For this cause"—that is, because of coming judgment, the Gospel
was preached. God wants the Gospel preached to all men. And if they
don't hear the Gospel or respond to the Gospel, He makes it very clear
that they are already dead in trespasses and sins, and they will be
judged as men in the flesh. But if they accept Christ, they can live
according to God in the Spirit. The Lord Jesus said in John 5:24, "Verily, verily, I say unto you, He that heareth my word, and believeth on

him that sent me, hath everlasting life, and shall not come into con-
demnation; but is passed from death unto life"—he was in a state of
death. He further amplified this thought at the time of the death of
Lazarus: "Jesus said unto her [Martha], I am the resurrection, and the
life: he that believeth in me, though he were *dead*, yet shall he live:
And whosoever liveth and believeth in me shall never die. Believest
thou this?" (John 11:25–26, italics mine). In other words, you and I
were *dead* in trespasses and sins. Paul meant the same thing when he
wrote to the Ephesians, "And you hath he quickened, who were dead
in trespasses and sins" (Eph. 2:1). We were spiritually dead. Paul went
on to say, "Wherein in time past ye walked according to the course of
this world. . . . fulfilling the desires of the flesh . . ." (Eph. 2:2–3).
Peter is saying the same thing here in this verse. The Gospel is being
preached, and when the Gospel is being preached, two things happen.
Some accept it, and if they accept it, they are going to live for God and
live throughout eternity. Others reject it, and those who reject the Gospel are the men who are dead in sins and are dead to God throughout
eternity; that is, they have no relation to Him whatsoever.

> **But the end of all things is at hand: be ye therefore sober,
> and watch unto prayer [1 Pet. 4:7].**

"But the end of all things is at hand." That has been true since the day
the Lord Jesus went back to heaven. Paul could say that the coming of
Christ was imminent: "Looking for that blessed hope, and the glorious
appearing of the great God and our Saviour Jesus Christ" (Titus 2:13).
Peter says, "The end of all things is at hand." God is going to bring this
world to a standstill one of these days while He judges it. He will take
His own out of the world, and there will be a lot of things to straighten
up in the lives of believers. They will go before the judgment seat of
Christ, not regarding salvation but regarding rewards, regarding the
life which they have lived for God. This is another reason we should
live for God—we are coming up for judgment.

"Be ye therefore sober. and watch unto prayer. "Sober" should be
translated "soberminded." Peter uses this expression a great deal. He
actually means, "Be ye therefore *intelligent*." Be an intelligent Chris-

tian. An intelligent Christian is one who knows the Bible; that is, he will know it the best he can. (I often make the confession that I marvel at my ignorance of the Word of God. The more I study it, the more I see how little I really know about the Word of God.) But, my friend, an intelligent, sober-minded Christian is going to know all he can about the Word of God.

The Christian is also to be intelligent in this evil world. The Lord Jesus said to His disciples, "Be ye therefore wise as serpents, and helpless as doves" (Matt. 10:16). You need to have the wisdom of a serpent today; if you don't, another snake around the corner is going to bite you, I can assure you of that!

"Watch unto prayer." In other words prayer should have in it that anticipation, that expectation of the coming of Christ. Our prayer meetings are dead today because we are not looking for Him. He is the *living* Christ. We ought to talk to Him now for we are going to talk to Him hereafter. And at the judgment He is going to talk to us—that is the thing I'm not so sure I'm looking forward to!

> **And above all things have fervent charity among yourselves: for charity shall cover the multitude of sins [1 Pet. 4:8].**

"Have fervent love among yourselves, for charity [love] shall cover the multitude of sins." Peter is talking about our relations as believers today. The writer of the Proverbs said, "Hatred stirreth up strifes: but love covereth all sins" (Prov. 10:12). Hatred in a church will stir up strife. This little clique will be against that little clique, and these folk will be against somebody else, and all that type of thing. But love covers up all that. Maybe you don't like the way your pastor combs his hair. I knew a pastor in Texas who told me that he had a lock of hair right on top of his head which would always stand up no matter how he combed it. He said that the choir threatened to quit because of it. They sat behind him and could always see that hair come up sometime during his sermon. They actually became angry with him because of that lock of hair. Every time he went for a haircut he had the barber cut it off because he did not want to offend his choir. Imagine that type of thing! If they had had love in their hearts, that lock of hair wouldn't have bothered them one bit.

> **Use hospitality one to another without grudging [1 Pet. 4:9].**

I think hospitality can also be expressed in ways other than entertaining in your home. The minister who is traveling and speaking in conferences needs to be alone. He and his wife need to have a room in a motel where he can study and pray rather than be in a home where he has to carry on conversation all the time. May I say, if you want to extend hospitality to your visiting speaker, take care of his motel bill. Maybe you could also invite him out for dinner.

"Without grudging." However we extend our hospitality, it should be done with real warmth.

> **As every man hath received the gift, even so minister the same one to another, as good stewards of the manifold grace of God [1 Pet. 4:10].**

"As every man hath received the gift"—"the gift" means a particular spiritual gift, and there are many gifts. Paul tells us in 1 Corinthians 12 that there is one body and many members and that the church is a body in which there are many members and many gifts. I don't know who you are, and I don't know what your gift is; I do know that if you are a child of God, you have some gift and you are to be using it in serving one another.

> **If any man speak, let him speak as the oracles of God; if any man minister, let him do it as of the ability which God giveth: that God in all things may be glorified through Jesus Christ, to whom be praise and dominion for ever and ever. Amen [1 Pet. 4:11].**

If a man is not speaking the Word of God, he has no business standing in the pulpit. We have no business saying we are teaching the Bible when we are not really teaching it.

"If any man minister, let him do it as of the ability which God giveth." In other words, here is one man who teaches the Bible one way and another who teaches it another way, and you say, "I like this one, and I don't like the other." Well, the other man's method may appeal to someone to whom your man doesn't appeal. We should let each one minister "as of the ability which God giveth."

"That God in all things may be glorified through Jesus Christ, to whom be praise and dominion for ever and ever. Amen." Peter says that we are to teach the Word of God in such a way that God may get glory through Jesus Christ.

Peter is now going to talk about a different type of suffering. The people to whom he was writing were now moving into the orbit of the hurricane of persecution which broke out during the reign of Nero. Nero had already begun the persecution of the Christians in Rome, and it was spreading out through the empire. Peter warns his people that they are moving into that orbit of suffering. Many of them would become martyrs. You and I may not become martyrs—I trust we won't—but we are going to suffer in this world, my friend.

> **Beloved, think it not strange concerning the fiery trial which is to try you, as though some strange thing happened unto you [1 Pet. 4:12].**

"Think it not *strange* concerning the fiery trial which is to try [test] you." When suffering comes most of us react as if it were something strange—we feel that nobody else has ever suffered like we have suffered. When I was a pastor in Cleburne, Texas, I went one day to a home on one side of the railroad tracks to visit a family in which there had just been a suicide. I went there to minister the Word to them. They said to me, "Dr. McGee, why in the world did this happen to us? No one has ever been called upon to suffer as we are suffering." When I left their home I crossed over to the "wrong side of the railroad tracks" to visit another family. They too had just had a suicide in the family. Do you know what they said to me? "Dr. McGee, why should this happen to us? No one has ever been called upon to go through anything like this." We all tend to think that our suffering is strange, that it is unlike anything that has been suffered before.

My friend, I do not know what your problem is, but I assure you that it is not something strange. Others have gone through the same thing, and you will never be the one who will suffer more than anyone else. When Paul was chosen as an apostle, the Lord said, ". . . I will shew him how great things he must suffer for my name's sake" (Acts 9:16). Paul has gone the limit of suffering; therefore you will not be going the limit, and you should not consider your suffering a strange thing. All of us fall into this fallacy in our thinking. I know that I could not believe it when the doctor told me that I had cancer. I thought you could have cancer, but I never thought I could have cancer. I thought that cancer was something for somebody else but not for me.

"The fiery trial which is to try [test] you" should be "which is *testing you*"—that is, it was going on right then—"as though some strange thing *was happening* unto you." These believers were already being tested by suffering. Suffering is not something which is accidental; it is the normal Christian experience. Peter says, "Don't think it's strange, because this is the normal experience of believers."

"Fiery trial" is literally *smelted in a furnace*. David spoke of the fact that God's testing of him was like putting silver into a furnace to purify it. We find this thought throughout all of Scripture. Peter has now mentioned this fiery trial several times. He had personally endured suffering, and he was yet to die a martyr's death by crucifixion.

This little poem expresses it the best—

> Out from the mine and the darkness,
>   Out from the damp and the mold,
> Out from the fiery furnace,
>   Cometh each grain of gold.
> Crushed into atoms and leveled
>   Down to the humblest dust
> With never a heart to pity,
>   With never a hand to trust.

Molten and hammered and beaten
    Seemeth it ne'er to be done.
Oh, for such fiery trial,
    What hath the poor gold done?
Oh, 'twere a mercy to leave it
    Down in the damp and the mold.
If this is the glory of living,
    Then better to be dross than gold.

Under the press and the roller,
    Into the jaws of the mint,
Stamped with the emblem of freedom,
    With never a flaw or a dint.
Oh, what a joy, the refining,
    Out of the damp and the mold.
And stamped with the glorious
      image,
    Oh, beautiful coin of gold!
             "In the Crucible"
             —Author unknown

God has a purpose in our suffering, my friend.

But rejoice, inasmuch as ye are partakers of Christ's sufferings; that, when his glory shall be revealed, ye may be glad also with exceeding joy [1 Pet. 4:13].

Why are we to rejoice in trials? Because suffering prepares us for the coming of Christ. Paul wrote in Romans 8:17, "And if children, then heirs; heirs of God, and joint-heirs with Christ; if so be that we suffer with him, that we may be also glorified together." I think we need to face up to the fact that there is no shortcut to living the Christian life. There is no easy way. Let me repeat, the Christian life is a banquet—because He has invited us to the table of salvation—but it is not a picnic. We are to suffer for Him and with Him. And we will know the reason for each testing when we stand in His presence someday. I tell you, I would be embarrassed to sit down with Paul in glory and be on the same level with him, because he suffered so much. And today some folk criticize Simon Peter, but we are also going to look up to him when we get to heaven. The Word of God makes it very clear that suffering is a part of the Christian life. Suffering is what develops you. We hear so much talk about how everything is supposed to be smooth and lovely in the Christian marriage and in the Christian home. My friend, I do not agree with that at all—sorrow and suffering will come to the Christian home. I know of nothing that drew my wife and me together like the death of our first little one. And believe me, we wanted that little one. We sat in that hospital room and simply wept and prayed together. That is still a sacred memory in our lives—it did something for us.

> **If ye be reproached for the name of Christ, happy are ye; for the spirit of glory and of God resteth upon you: on their part he is evil spoken of, but on your part he is glorified [1 Pet. 4:14].**

This is strange language, whether it is in the Greek or in the English. "If you are reproached for the name of Christ, you ought to rejoice in it," Peter says.

"For the spirit of glory and of God resteth upon you." Again may I say, suffering is a token that you are a child of God. The greatest proof that you are a child of God is that you can endure suffering. If you are being carried around on a silver platter with a silver spoon in your mouth, you must not be God's child because that is not the way He does things.

"On their part he is evil spoken of, but on your part he is glorified." You can glorify God whatever comes. It is said that during the devastating San Francisco earthquake of 1906 there was a dear, wonderful Christian lady who came out and was singing praises to God. Everybody else was crying, and some were praying for the first time in their lives. Someone asked her, "What do you mean by singing praises to God at a time like this?" She replied, "I thank God that I have a God

who is strong enough to shake this little earth!" I say "amen" to that.
However there are very few people who could praise God during the
time of an earthquake.

> **But let none of you suffer as a murderer, or as a thief, or
> as an evildoer, or as a busybody in other men's matters
> [1 Pet. 4:15].**

Peter puts murder right down with gossiping and criticizing others; he
makes no distinction between them at all. Paul did the same thing.
Actually, Paul and Peter and James agree on everything. They are all
preaching the same gospel that produces the same kind of a life.

Peter says that we ought not to be suffering for our own sins. God
never tests you with sin, my friend; He never tests you with evil, as
James makes clear to us in his epistle. Peter says, "Let none of you
suffer as a murderer."

> **Yet if any man suffer as a Christian, let him not be
> ashamed; but let him glorify God on this behalf [1 Pet.
> 4:16].**

My heart goes out to the Christian who is in prison today because he is
truly suffering punishment. However, if he is suffering because of his
own sin, he cannot glorify God for the fact that he is in prison, but he
can glorify the Lord and witness for Him in the midst of it.

> **For the time is come that judgment must begin at the
> house of God: and if it first begin at us, what shall the
> end be of them that obey not the gospel of God? [1 Pet.
> 4:17].**

"For the time is come that judgment must begin at the house of God."
Believers are going to appear before the judgment seat of Christ. Paul
wrote, "For we must all appear before the judgment seat of Christ; that
every one may receive the things done in his body, according to that he
hath done, whether it be good or bad" (2 Cor. 5:10). "We"—Paul is
talking about Christians. "That every one may receive the things done
in his body"—that is, the things done while you were living down

here. "According to that he hath done, whether it be good or bad"—we all must come before Christ's judgment seat.

Peter continues, "If it first begin at us, what shall the end be of them that obey not the gospel of God?" Christ has paid the penalty for our sins, but suppose that we have lived a life that has not brought glory to Him? My friend, we are to be judged. And if God is going to judge His own, what about the lost world which would not hear or obey the Gospel of God?

> **And if the righteous scarcely be saved, where shall the ungodly and the sinner appear? [1 Pet. 4:18].**

In other words, we as believers just barely made it. The righteous are saved only by the death of Christ and their faith in Christ. That is the only way we ever got saved, and we just barely made it, my friend. During a recent period of physical recuperation, my wife and I reminisced about our past lives. We really got acquainted in new ways, and I kidded her, "My, I'm just now coming to know you." I think maybe we ought to get married now that I know you!" But I also said to her, "When I look back at my life, how I started out on the wrong track, the wrong foot, it is nothing but a miracle that God ever saved me. I just marvel at it. I just barely made it."

John Wesley spoke of himself as "a brand plucked from the burning," and that is true of most of us. When John Wesley came to America, he was not saved, he was not a Christian. He made this statement, "I came to America to convert Indians, but who is going to convert John Wesley?" His biographer tells us that at the governor's court in Georgia he met one of the noblemen of Great Britain who had been sent over to administer that area. He was a very wealthy man with a name, and he had married a beautiful, young wife. That young woman and John Wesley began to eye each other, and evidently John Wesley fell in love with her. He asked her to leave and go with him to live among the Indians. And he thought he was a Christian and a missionary! But she sent him back to England, saying, "John this won't work. I love you, and I'll always love you, but God has called you to do something for Him." She evidently was a Christian, and so she sent him back to England. It is said that three times he started up the gangplank, and three times he started to walk back. But she motioned him to go, and he went back to England. One night walking down Aldersgate, he went upstairs and heard a man speaking on Galatians. Later, he could write in his journal, "I felt my heart strangely warmed. I felt that I did trust Christ, Christ alone, for my salvation, and there was given to me an assurance that He had forgiven me of my sins."

Now if the righteous scarcely be saved, if they be but brands plucked from the burning, "where shall the ungodly and the sinner appear?" Peter asks. My friend, if you are not a Christian, and if Vernon McGee just barely made it and made it only by trusting Christ, how do you think you are going to make it? There is not but one hope—there is only one way of salvation. The Lord Jesus said, "I am the way" (see John 14:6).

Wherefore let them that suffer according to the will of God commit the keeping of their souls to him in well-doing, as unto a faithful Creator [1 Pet. 4:19].

Those who have really suffered know what it is to commit themselves to God. Paul spoke of this when he said, ". . . I know whom I have believed, and am persuaded that he is able to keep that which I have committed unto him against that day" (2 Tim. 1:12). What had Paul committed unto Him? Some people believe this refers to the gospel which God committed to Paul. I'll agree with that, but I think the deeper meaning is that Paul is saying, "I came to Christ and simply committed everything to Him. I made a deposit. What things were gain to me I counted loss, and what was loss became gain to me, in order that I might win Christ." Paul listed about eight different things that he formerly trusted for his salvation (see Phil. 3:1–6). Then he said, "But what things were gain to me, those I counted loss for Christ. Yea doubtless, and I count all things but loss for the excellency of the knowledge of Christ Jesus my Lord: for whom I have suffered the loss of all things, and do count them but dung, that I may win Christ" (Phil. 3:7–8). In effect, he was saying, "I flushed all that down; I trusted that no longer. I only trusted Christ."

Peter says, "Let them that suffer . . . commit the keeping of their souls to him." Have you really trusted Him? You probably have a safety deposit box in which you keep your valuables. When you go to sleep at night, you don't worry about them at all. My friend, I went to sleep last night, and I didn't worry about Vernon McGee's soul. Do you know why? I went to sleep last night in peace because Christ has taken care of all that. I've made my deposit with Him, and I trust Him today. Have you made a deposit with Him? Have you committed your soul to Him? May I say, if you have done that, even when trouble comes to you, even when the dark day comes, even when you are called to go down through the valley, you can do it knowing that He will take care of you.

God hath not promised skies always blue,
　Flower-strewn pathways all our lives through;
God hath not promised sun without rain,
　Joy without sorrow, peace without pain.

God hath not promised we shall not know
　Toil and temptation, trouble and woe;
He hath not told us we shall not bear
　Many a burden, many a care.

God hath not promised smooth roads and wide,
　Swift, easy travel, needing no guide;
Never a mountain, rocky and steep,
　Never a river, turbid and deep.

But God hath promised strength for the day,
　Rest for the laborer, light for the way,
Grace for the trials, help from above,
　Unfailing sympathy, undying love.
　　　　　"God Hath Not Promised"
　　　　　—Annie Johnson Flint

Have you made your deposit, my friend? Have you committed your soul unto Him?

CHAPTER 5

THEME: Suffering and the second coming of Christ
produce service and hope, humility and patience

SUFFERING AND THE SECOND COMING
OF CHRIST

In this final chapter of 1 Peter, suffering and the second coming of Christ are brought together. What is the relation of our suffering to the second coming of Christ? The Christian life began for each of us with the suffering of the Lord Jesus Christ on the cross where He bore the penalty of our sins. There is also suffering in the life of the child of God today because God uses suffering in our lives to sharpen us and to make us the kind of Christians that He wants and that He can use. I have divided this chapter into two sections: Verses 1–4 teach that suffering produces service and hope; verses 5–14 teach that suffering produces humility and patience.

We have, therefore, the suffering of Christ in the past and the present suffering of the saints, and then we have the second coming of Christ. Every Christian ought to have the second coming of Christ in his plan and his program for the future. We are often told that we need to have a life plan. Is the second coming of Christ—when He comes to take you out of the world and then returns with you to reign on the earth—a part of your program? Or is it some ethereal, ephemeral thing which hangs out there in space like a will-o'-the-wisp that really has no meaning in your life at all? His second coming is not just a doctrine; it is something which enters into our lives. There is nothing which will buoy you up in time of trouble and suffering like the *reality* of the second coming of Christ. I am going to see Him some day; I am going to come into His presence! What a time of real blessing that will be, and Peter tells us that our present suffering is related to that.

SUFFERING PRODUCES SERVICE AND HOPE

**The elders which are among you I exhort, who am also
an elder, and a witness of the sufferings of Christ, and**

also a partaker of the glory that shall be revealed [1 Pet. 5:1].

Peter begins by asserting his position; however, he doesn't call himself even an apostle here. He is speaking of the fact that he is an elder—"who am also an elder." That means there were other men who were elders. The Greek word used here, *presbuteros*, is a word which is sometimes used in speaking of a person being an elder or elder person. The Greek word which is translated "bishop" is *episkopos*, and it speaks of the office of the man, not the person of the man. It is the spiritual office of shepherding; the same word is used for "shepherd." This is all that Simon Peter ever claimed to be—he calls himself a fellow elder. He never claimed a superior place above his brethren, but as a fellow elder he exhorts them.

"And a witness of the sufferings of Christ." Peter was in a unique position because he was a witness of the sufferings of Christ.

"And also a partaker of the glory that shall be revealed." In the past Peter saw that glory. In his second epistle, Peter identifies this as taking place on the Mount of Transfiguration. Peter saw Him die yonder on Mount Calvary, and he saw Him transfigured yonder on the Mount of Transfiguration. That mount was probably in the north, and I have always felt that Mount Hermon could have been the place, although the geographical location is not important. What took place there is important, and Peter says that he was a witness of it. However, there is a glory that is coming in the future which will be greater than that—"the glory that shall be revealed."

Feed the flock of God which is among you, taking the oversight thereof, not by constraint, but willingly; not for filthy lucre, but of a ready mind [1 Pet. 5:2].

Peter is emphasizing the fact that an elder, occupying the office of a bishop (elders are never spoken of in the singular, there was never to be only one), is to be the shepherd of a flock. Shepherding suggests provision and protection, supervision and discipline, instruction and direction. The ministry of an elder is to be performed in a very positive way, but Peter also gives a negative injunction.

First of all, Peter says that elders are to minister for the right reason, in the right spirit, not because they *must* do it but because they freely choose to do so. Will you notice what he says: "Feed the flock of God which is among you, taking the oversight thereof, not by constraint, but *willingly*." Do it willingly. God doesn't want you to take an office in the church in this pouting spirit: "Well, if you can't get anybody else to do it, I'll do it." My friend, don't you do it, because that is not the reason to serve Him. There is no value in serving Him if you are doing it under constraint. "Not for filthy lucre but of a ready mind." Peter makes it clear that there must not only be the right reason—the right spirit, because they freely choose to serve—but there must also be the right motive for service. It is not to be for material gain but for the sheer delight of doing it. An elder is to find satisfaction in the job itself rather than in what he gets out of it.

A number of years ago my daughter and I were driving the freeway into Los Angeles together since she also had a job with the church that I was then serving as pastor. As usual, we got stuck in the traffic on the freeway. I said to her, "Look around at these people. Do you see anybody who looks happy? There they sit, under tension and pressure, trying to get to a job which they despise. Most people today are doing a job they do not like to do at all. It's wonderful to be in the Lord's service where you can do your job because you love to do it and you want to do it." That has made the ministry of teaching the Word of God a sheer joy to me. Simon Peter says that there must be a right motive in Christian service.

Neither as being lords over God's heritage, but being en- samples to the flock [1 Pet. 5:3].

In other words, an elder should exercise his ministry in the right manner, not driving but leading, not domineering but setting an example. It is a work, therefore, in which he ought to be an example to the flock. I do not think that a preacher should get into the pulpit and browbeat his congregation to do something that he actually is not doing himself. I made it a practice never to ask my congregation to give to any cause to which I didn't also give. I do not think we have a right to make a demand of other folk that we are not doing ourselves.

And when the chief Shepherd shall appear, ye shall receive a crown of glory that fadeth not away [1 Pet. 5:4].

An elder's ministry should be done with the proper awareness that he serves the Chief Shepherd to whom he is answerable and who will Himself reward his service with rewards which are eternal. Don't get the impression that we are working for nothing. We are not. Paul made it clear that a Christian is not to work for nothing. You are to work for Him and look to Him for a reward some day. That is the way we are to serve Him.

"Ye shall receive a crown of glory that fadeth not away." There are many crowns mentioned in Scripture, including the crown of life and the crown of righteousness. What is a crown of glory? I believe that it means we are going to share some day in His glory.

In a study I made many years ago, I found about a dozen different words in the Old Testament which were translated by the word glory. Glory is a word that is often used today. What do you understand by the word glory? How big is glory? What shape is it? What color it is? What is glory? I suspect that the average Christian would have nothing but the foggiest notion about the meaning of glory.

I have found that glory does have shape and size. Listen to the Word of God: "The heavens declare the glory of God; and the firmament sheweth his handiwork" (Ps.19:1). The size of the universe, as determined by our scientific measurements, is staggering yet is probably only the front yard of God's great universe. That is glory—the greatness of our God.

What about the color of glory? Look up at this vast universe at night; look up at the sky. And look at the earth. In the fall, especially if you live in New England, take a good look at the leaves on the trees. It is wonderful to be in that part of the country and to see all the color. That's glory—the glory of God. I know a retired man who lives here in

Southern California, and he raises some of the most beautiful roses and zinnias I have ever seen. Oh, are they colorful! One time while I was visiting him in his garden, he reached down and lifted up the head of one of those zinnias, and he said, "In the springtime I simply put a little seed in the ground. Look at what has come up! And then they try to tell me there is no God!" Glory has color, my friend.

May I say to you, God's glory is something that is quite wonderful, and we are going to share in that some day. He calls it a crown of glory.

Peter calls Him "the chief Shepherd" here. The Good Shepherd gives His life for the sheep—that is seen in Psalm 22. The Great Shepherd watches over the sheep—that is seen in Psalm 23. In Psalm 24 He is the Chief Shepherd who is coming again. Some day our Chief Shepherd is going to appear, and He will still have with Him His flock, and we will be members of that flock. How wonderful this is!

SUFFERING PRODUCES HUMILITY AND PATIENCE

Likewise, ye younger, submit yourselves unto the elder. Yea, all of you be subject one to another, and be clothed with humility: for God resisteth the proud, and giveth grace to the humble.

Humble yourselves therefore under the mighty hand of God, that he may exalt you in due time [1 Pet. 5:5–6].

"Likewise, ye younger, submit yourselves unto the elder." This has been reversed in our day—today the elder is supposed to submit to the younger. Young people are the ones who are protesting, and they are the ones who want to discard the establishment. However, the Christian young person needs to realize that the Word of God says, "Ye younger, submit yourselves unto the elder." After all, your father, if you have a good or a godly father, has a lot of sense and maybe more sense than you have.

A friend of mine told me, "I was ashamed of my dad at the time when I went away to college. Although he had made good money, and he was an executive, I was ashamed of him. He had such old-fashioned ideas; he was a real square. When I finished college and got out in the business world, I didn't see him for a couple of years. When I did see him again, I was absolutely amazed to see how much he'd learned in just six years!" A lot of young people find out, after they themselves have been out in the school of hard knocks for awhile, that their dads have learned a great deal.

"Yea, all of you be subject one to another." In other words, believers should not insist on having their way over others.

"And be *clothed* with humility." Actually, we are to be armed with it; that is the picture that is given here.

"For God resisteth the proud and giveth grace to the humble." Peter has talked a great deal about humility and about grace. A proud person will not be able to experience the grace of God. It is only when you and I come in humility that we will be able to grow the grace of God.

"Humble yourselves therefore under the mighty hand of God, that he may exalt you in due time." In view of the coming of Christ, humility should be the attitude of the child of God. Christ is the one who will establish justice and make things right when He comes. You cannot straighten out this world, although you may think you can.

Casting all your care upon him; for he careth for you [1 Pet. 5:7].

"He careth for you" literally means that it matters to Him concerning you. Peter is talking about anxiety. The Lord Jesus said, "Come unto Me all ye that labor and are heavy laden, and I will rest you" (see Matt. 11:28). Bring your burden of sins to Him, and He will save you. Then come to Him later on, and He will meet you and help you with your problems. Cast your care upon Him. Paul told the Philippian believers, "Worry about nothing; pray about everything." That is, take it to the Lord in prayer, and leave it there—don't pick it up again.

Be sober, be vigilant; because your adversary the devil, as a roaring lion, walketh about, seeking whom he may devour [1 Pet. 5:8].

The word *sober* is from a different Greek word than that used in 1 Peter 4:7. Here the word means "to be watchful."

"Be sober, be vigilant, because your adversary the devil, as a roaring lion, walketh about, seeking whom he may devour." We are told to resist Satan; the Devil is loose in the world today.

> **Whom resist stedfast in the faith, knowing that the same afflictions are accomplished in your brethren that are in the world [1 Pet. 5:9].**

"Whom resist stedfast in the faith." The picture here is of an army standing against an enemy. We should stand with other believers. I do not think you can resist the Devil by yourself. You not only need the armor of God, but you will also need other believers to stand with you. That is the reason that whenever I have need, I let all the listeners to my radio broadcast know about it. I want them to stand with me in prayer—we need to do that. "Whom resist stedfast in the faith, knowing that the same afflictions are accomplished in your brethren that are in the world."

> **But the God of all grace, who hath called us unto his eternal glory by Christ Jesus, after that ye have suffered a while, make you perfect, stablish, strengthen, settle you [1 Pet. 5:10].**

"But the God of all grace. who hath called us unto his eternal glory by Christ Jesus"—that is, "*in* Christ Jesus." We will have no glory in ourselves. The church is sort of like the moon which simply reflects the light of the sun. Our glory will be only reflected glory, but we in Christ are going to share in that glory. Actually, the word *Jesus* is not in the better manuscripts; rather, this is that phrase which we often find in the New Testament—"in Christ."

"After that ye have suffered a while, make you perfect"—that is, bring you to perfection. "Stablish, strengthen"—the Lord Jesus told Simon Peter to strengthen the brethren (see Luke 22:32). "Settle you"—that means to restore you.

> To him be glory and dominion for ever and ever. Amen
> [1 Pet. 5:11].

This is the benediction. And then Peter adds a little P.S.—

> By Silvanus, a faithful brother unto you, as I suppose, I
> have written briefly, exhorting, and testifying that this is
> the true grace of God wherein ye stand [1 Pet. 5:12].

Peter is the author, but Silvanus wrote this for him. If you don't like the
quality of the Greek here, blame Silvanus.

> The church that is at Babylon, elected together with
> you, saluteth you; and so doth Marcus my son [1 Pet.
> 5:13].

"The church that is at Babylon, elected together with you, saluteth
you." I think "Babylon" here means Babylon, although some think it is
a figurative name for Rome. Simon Peter is too practical to have used a
figurative term.

"And so doth Marcus my son." Marcus is John Mark, the writer of
the Gospel of Mark, who was not Peter's natural son but his son in the
faith. Although at one time Paul would not take him along on a missionary journey, Mark made good.

> Greet ye one another with a kiss of charity. Peace be
> with you all that are in Christ Jesus. Amen [1 Pet. 5:14].

"Greet ye one another with a kiss of charity." Someone has said, "A
kiss to a young girl is hope, to a married woman is faith, but to an old
maid is charity." In our country and culture, I think we had better just
use the handshake as the means of Christian greeting.

This is Peter's final benediction: "Peace be with you all that are in
Christ Jesus. Amen."

BIBLIOGRAPHY
(Recommended for Further Study)

Barbieri, Louis A. *First and Second Peter*. Chicago, Illinois: Moody Press, 1977. (Fine, inexpensive survey)

English, E. Schuyler. *The Life and Letters of St. Peter*. New York, New York: Our Hope, 1941. (Excellent)

Hiebert, D. Edmond. *The Epistle of 1 Peter*. Chicago, Illinois: Moody Press, 1983. (Excellent, comprehensive treatment)

Ironside, H. A. *Notes on James and Peter*. Neptune, New Jersey: Loizeaux Brothers, n.d.

Kelly, William. *The Epistles of Peter*. Addison, Illinois: Bible Truth Publishers, n.d.

Leighton, Robert. *A Practical Commentary on First Peter*. Grand Rapids, Michigan: Kregel Publications, 1845.

Lumby, J. Rawson. *The Epistles of Peter*. (Expositor's Bible.) Grand Rapids, Michigan: Wm. B. Eerdmans Publishing Company, 1943.

Meyer, F. B. *Tried by Fire* (1 Peter). Fort Washington, Pennsylvania: Christian Literature Crusade, n.d. (Rich, devotional study)

Robertson, A. T. *Epochs in the Life of Simon Peter*. Grand Rapids, Michigan: Baker Book House, n.d.

Stibbs, Alan. *The First Epistle General of Peter*. Grand Rapids, Michigan: Wm. B. Eerdmans Publishing Company, 1959.

Thomas, W. H. Griffith. *The Apostle Peter*. Grand Rapids, Michigan: Wm. B. Eerdmans Publishing Company, 1956. (Excellent)

Wolston, W. T. P. *Simon Peter—His Life and Letters.* London, England: James Nisbet and Company, 1896. (Excellent)

Wuest, Kenneth S. *Wuest's Word Studies from the Greek New Testament for English Readers.* Grand Rapids, Michigan: Wm. B. Eerdmans Publishing Co., 1942. (1 Peter)